Can you GET music on the MOON?

## PUFFIN BOOKS

UK | USA | Canada | Ireland | Australia
India | New Zealand | South Africa

Puffin Books is part of the Penguin Random House group of companies whose addresses can be found at global.penguinrandomhouse.com

www.penguin.co.uk   www.puffin.co.uk   www.ladybird.co.uk

First published 2025
001

Text copyright © Dr Sheila Kanani, 2025
Illustrations copyright © Liz Kay, 2025

The moral right of the author and illustrator has been asserted

Penguin Random House values and supports copyright. Copyright fuels creativity, encourages diverse voices, promotes freedom of expression and supports a vibrant culture. Thank you for purchasing an authorized edition of this book and for respecting intellectual property laws by not reproducing, scanning or distributing any part of it by any means without permission. You are supporting authors and enabling Penguin Random House to continue to publish books for everyone. No part of this book may be used or reproduced in any manner for the purpose of training artificial intelligence technologies or systems. In accordance with Article 4(3) of the DSM Directive 2019/790, Penguin Random House expressly reserves this work from the text and data mining exception.

Design by Beth Free, Studio Nic&Lou
Printed and bound in China

The authorized representative in the EEA is Penguin Random House Ireland, Morrison Chambers, 32 Nassau Street, Dublin D02 YH68

A CIP catalogue record for this book is available from the British Library

ISBN: 978-0-241-52216-5

All correspondence to:
Puffin Books
Penguin Random House Children's
One Embassy Gardens, 8 Viaduct Gardens, London SW11 7BW

# Can you GET Music on the MOON?

The AMAZING science of SOUND and SPACE!

## DR SHEILA KANANI
*Illustrated by Liz Kay*

- **2** INTRODUCTION
- **16** SOUND IN SCIENCE AND TECHNOLOGY
- **26** SOUND IN MUSIC AND PERFORMANCE
- **42** SOUND IN THE ANIMAL KINGDOM
- **56** SOUND ON THE EARTH
- **66** SOUND IN THE SEA
- **80** SOUND IN THE SKY
- **94** SOUND IN SPACE
- **114** SO, CAN YOU GET MUSIC ON THE MOON?
- **118** GLOSSARY

# A UNIVERSE FULL OF SOUNDS!

You might have come across the saying that in space no one can hear you scream, but do you know what that means? Or whether it is even true? In this book, you'll discover the answers to these questions and many more about sound, space and nature.

Together, we'll zoom across the stars, dive deep into the oceans and even drill far below ground to see how sound changes in different environments. We'll find out how humans first started playing and recording music, listen for patterns in whale song, and discover whether mice really are as quiet as everyone says. We'll be amazed by cutting-edge sound technology, learn why we see lightning before hearing thunder, and investigate eerie sounds at the bottom of the sea. And, when we get to space, we'll wonder what aliens might sound like – and discover, once and for all, whether or not we can get music on the Moon!

But first, let's find out a bit more about how sound works, how we hear, and why sound can make us feel certain things.

INTRODUCTION

3

# WHAT IS SOUND?

Vibrate means to move quickly back and forth.

Sound is a type of energy that is created when an object vibrates.

For example, when a person knocks on a door, it makes the door vibrate. The vibrations are too small for our eyes to see, but they cause the particles in the air near the door to vibrate too. These particles then cause the particles next to them to vibrate as well, setting off a chain reaction of vibrations!

> Atoms are the basic building blocks of matter. They join together with other atoms – a bit like LEGO™ blocks! – to make up matter. For example, a piece of iron is a type of matter, and it's made up of lots of iron atoms all joined together.
>
> When two or more atoms join together, they make a molecule. A molecule is the smallest possible unit of a substance. For example, one water molecule is the smallest unit of water. (The water molecule is made up of three atoms – two hydrogen atoms and one oxygen atom.)
>
> The word particle can refer to both atoms and molecules, but we generally use it to refer to the smallest possible piece of something. So, a water particle is just another way of describing a water molecule.

The vibrations travel through the air as waves of energy that reach our ears, and we hear these waves as sound. The substance that the sound-waves travel through is called the medium, and it could be a gas (like air) or a solid (like a table) or a liquid (like the sea). Once the waves run out of energy, we can't hear them any more.

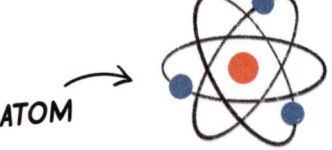

ATOM

## THE SHAPE OF A SOUND-WAVE

Sound-waves are longitudinal waves. This means that all the particles in the medium vibrate in the same direction as the movement of the wave. It's helpful to think of this movement like a Slinky going down the stairs. The Slinky moves by stretching apart, then squashing together, with each coil pulling the one behind it forwards. In a sound-wave, the particles act like the coils in the Slinky. The scientific word for this stretching is rarefaction, and the squashing is compression.

Amplitude is a measure of the height of a wave. The greater the amplitude, or the stronger the vibration, the louder the sound. For example, if you're playing a guitar and pluck a string hard, it will vibrate harder and make a louder sound than a string plucked gently.

If you are really far away from the object making the vibration, the sound becomes fainter by the time the vibrations reach you, because the sound-wave loses energy and vibrates less the further it travels.

Wavelength is the distance between the highest point of each wave, and frequency is how many waves fit into one second. The shorter the wavelength, the higher the frequency. The longer the wavelength, the lower the frequency. At higher frequencies, the particles in the medium (such as the air) vibrate very quickly, and this creates a high-pitched noise. An example of a high-frequency sound is a mouse's squeak. Meanwhile, low-frequency waves vibrate more slowly, and therefore create low-pitched noises, such as thunder.

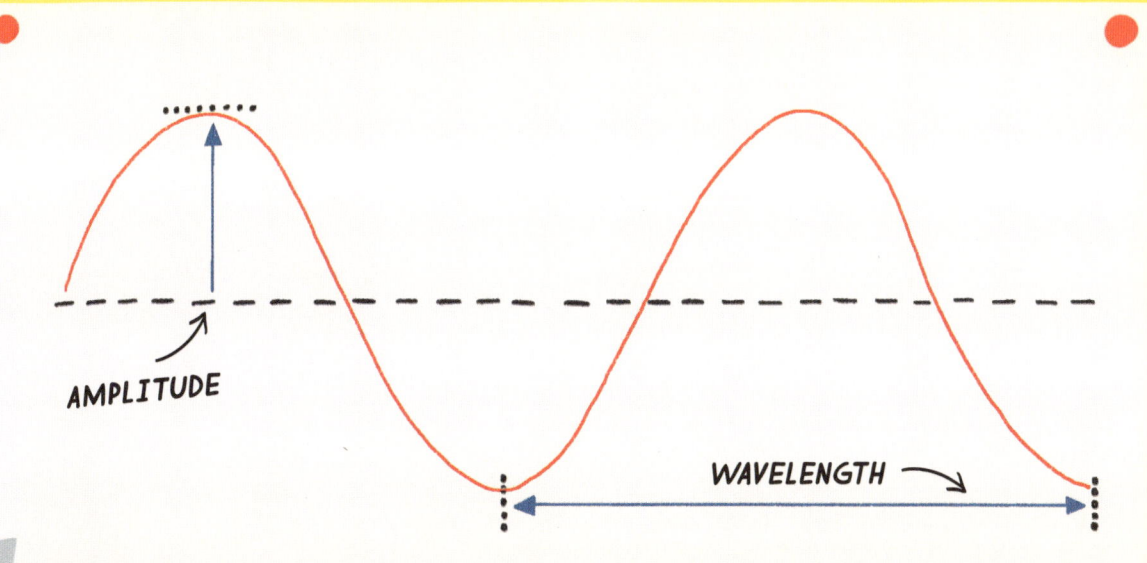

# SOUNDS IN DIFFERENT MEDIUMS

Density is a way of describing how many particles (or molecules) there are in a given area. If you fill a bottle with water, it will contain hundreds more particles of water than it did air when it was empty. This is because the water particles are packed closer together than the air particles so the water bottle is denser.

Do sounds move slower or faster when they travel through water? You might think the water would slow the vibrations down . . . but, actually, the opposite is true!

*In a solid, the particles are very tightly packed and fixed in place.*

*In a liquid, the particles are closer together and can still move around, but not as easily.*

*In a gas, such as the air, the particles are very loosely packed and can move around freely.*

Sound travels faster in a solid than in a liquid or in the air. This is because the particles in a solid are packed really tightly, so they can bump into each other more easily and the vibrations travel more quickly.

Sound travels faster in liquids than in air because the particles are closer together.

The speed of sound in air is faster in the summer than it is in the winter, because temperature affects the speed of sound. The warmer it is, the faster the particles can vibrate.

Since sound needs particles to vibrate, if there are no particles, there can be no sound. This means that in a vacuum (a place with no particles in it – not even air) sound can't travel. Outer space is a vacuum, so in outer space sound can't travel!

## ECHO ... ECHO ... ECHO ...

Sound-waves can be reflected, refracted and diffracted.

A sound-wave is reflected when it bounces off a surface and travels back to your ears, and you can hear the sound as an echo.

Sound can also be refracted, or bent, when it travels from one medium to another, for example, from a liquid to a solid.

If sound is travelling and meets an obstacle, such as a tree or the corner of a room, it can be diffracted, or spread out and change direction.

# HOW DO WE HEAR?

> The first bone is called the malleus or hammer, and is attached to the eardrum.
>
> The malleus is connected to the second bone, which is called the incus or anvil.
>
> The incus is also attached to the third bone, the stapes or stirrup.

So, what happens after an object makes a vibration? How do we actually *hear* the sound? Well, the vibrating air particles, or sound-waves, reach our ears and create a knock-on effect.

## STEP ONE:

The sound-waves enter the outer ear, called the pinna, which is the flappy bit on the outside of your head. Sound-waves enter the wider end of the pinna, and are directed towards the narrower end, where they enter the ear canal. The shape of the pinna amplifies the sound, or makes it louder (a bit like a mini megaphone!).

## STEP TWO:

The sound-waves enter the middle ear, where they bounce against the eardrum. The eardrum is a paper-thin layer that vibrates when the sound hits it. It's connected to three small bones in the middle ear, called the ossicles: the malleus, incus and stapes.

As the eardrum vibrates, it causes the ossicles to vibrate too. The stapes is connected to the final part of the middle ear – the oval window. The oval window is a bit like the eardrum, but smaller. The vibrating bones make the oval window vibrate, which amplifies the sound again!

## STEP THREE:

The vibrating oval window presses against the inner ear, or cochlea. The cochlea is shaped like a snail shell and full of tiny hairs. As the sound-waves pass over these hairs, the hairs respond to the vibrations and translate them into electrical signals, which travel along a path of nerves to the brain.

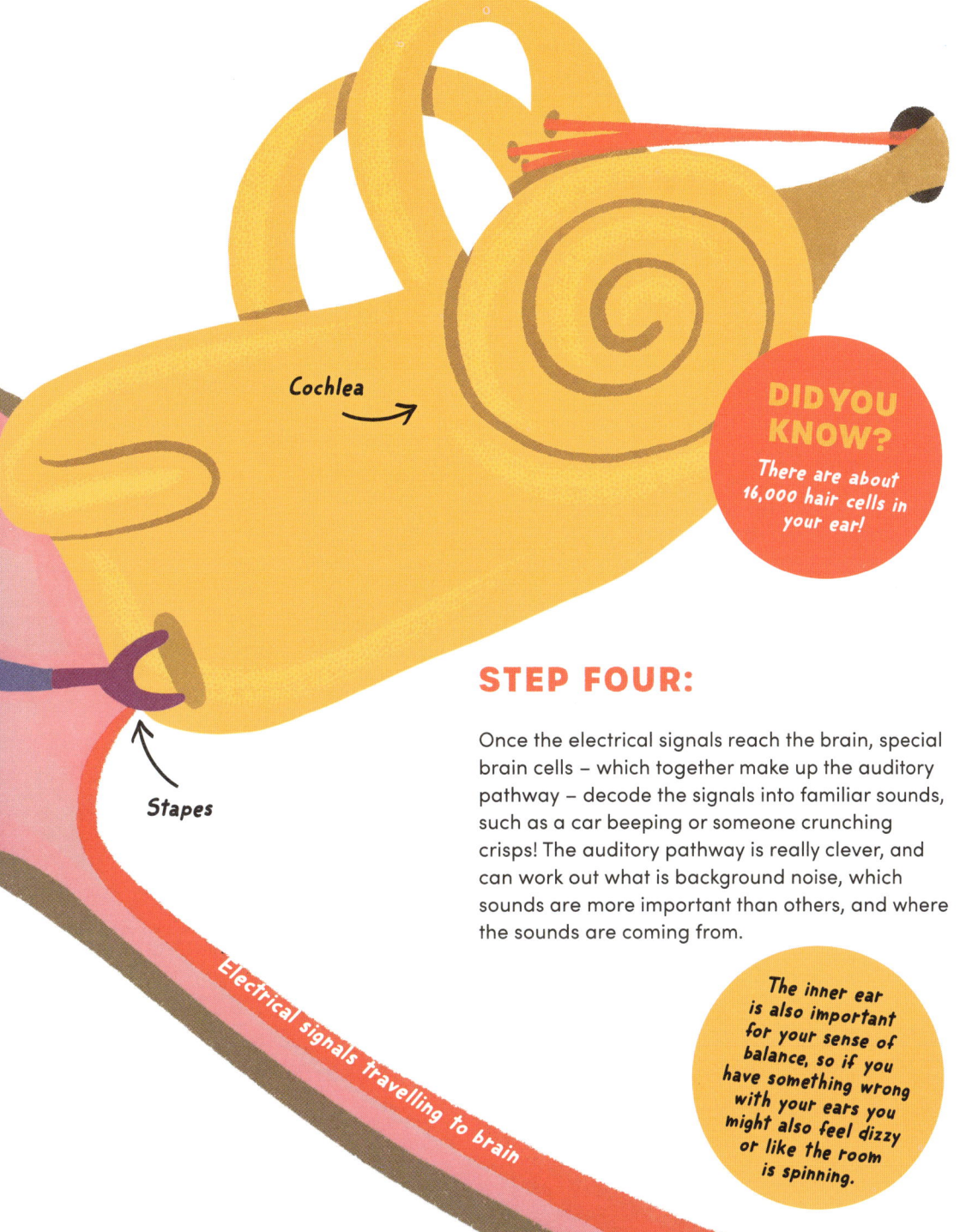

Cochlea

Stapes

Electrical signals travelling to brain

**DID YOU KNOW?**
There are about 16,000 hair cells in your ear!

## STEP FOUR:

Once the electrical signals reach the brain, special brain cells – which together make up the auditory pathway – decode the signals into familiar sounds, such as a car beeping or someone crunching crisps! The auditory pathway is really clever, and can work out what is background noise, which sounds are more important than others, and where the sounds are coming from.

The inner ear is also important for your sense of balance, so if you have something wrong with your ears you might also feel dizzy or like the room is spinning.

# CHANGES IN HEARING

The ear is like a machine, with lots of tiny working parts. As we get older, some parts of the machine can get worn out, so it doesn't work as well. Over time, we lose our ability to hear high-pitched noises, as the inner ear becomes less sensitive, and our hearing may get weaker. One reason for this is that the hair cells in the cochlea become damaged, and can no longer transmit electrical signals to the brain. But it isn't just age that can affect our hearing – not everyone is born with the same hearing abilities and there may be other reasons that people lose their hearing, or have different hearing abilities to begin with.

## HEARING DEVICES

If someone has permanent hearing loss, they might be offered hearing aids or a cochlear implant. A hearing aid is a small device that is worn on or near the ears to make sounds louder and clearer. Hearing aids don't make the wearer's hearing perfect, but they can amplify everyday sounds and improve the wearer's ability to hear speech.

Cochlear implants are used by people with severe hearing loss. Unlike hearing aids, which amplify sounds, they actually create the sensation of hearing. They are made up of two parts – one piece is worn behind the ear, and the other piece is implanted beneath the skin close to the ear.

*Acoustic sound is any type of sound that is within the human hearing frequency range.*

> Sound ranges are referred to by their frequency, and frequency is measured in hertz (Hz), with 1000 Hz being equal to 1 kilohertz (kHz). People above the age of twenty-five generally can't hear sounds that are above 15 kHz. A mosquito may buzz at 17.5 kHz, so older adults can't hear them!
>
> The human hearing frequency range can go up to 28 kHz and down to 12 Hz, but speech and communication frequencies range between 8 kHz and 250 Hz. Human hearing is no match for dogs, who can hear up to 50 kHz, or bats, who can hear even higher sounds – up to 110 kHz!

**HERE'S HOW A COCHLEAR IMPLANT WORKS:**

- Sounds are detected by the microphone on the external part of the ear, and converted into signals. These signals are sent through the skin by radio waves, and picked up by the receiver inside the person's head – which is held in place by magnets!

- The receiver sends electrical signals down a wire into electrodes, small pieces of metal that carry an electric current into materials that aren't metal, which are implanted in the cochlea.

- This causes the nerves in the cochlea to create electrical signals that travel to the brain, which translates them into sound.

Cochlear implant

The sound heard through a cochlear implant is not the same as sound heard through natural hearing, but over time the brain adapts to this new way of hearing.

INTRODUCTION

# MEASURING NOISE

Noise is measured in decibels. The faintest sound humans can hear is 1 decibel (dB), and sounds such as whispers and soft music are around 30 dB. A vacuum cleaner can be 70 dB, a noisy café comes in at 80 dB, someone shouting can be 90 dB and a rock concert can be 120 dB! Sounds above 85 dB can be harmful to our ears, so it's best to avoid listening to very loud sounds for long periods of time.

## BLAST OFF!

A rocket launch is one of the loudest noises in the world. The *Saturn V* rocket, which was used to send astronauts to the Moon, was reported to have generated a massive 204 dB! Since they are so incredibly loud, rocket launches can be dangerous for wildlife in the surrounding area. One solution is to build soundproof shelters for animals to hide in during launches – for example, soundproof nesting boxes for birds and specially built burrows for otters!

> According to tests carried out in 2021, the Orfield Anechoic Chamber in Minneapolis, in the United States of America, is the quietest place in the world, with a background noise reading of −24.9 dB.

## WHAT IS NOISE POLLUTION?

Sounds are all around us, but sometimes they get too loud or go on for too long, and that's when they become noise pollution. This is sound that is so loud or intense it can harm those who hear it. Any noises can be classed as pollution! For instance, some people love using fireworks for special celebrations, but if the fireworks went on all year they could damage people's ears, stop them from sleeping and harm their health.

## THE IMPACTS OF NOISE POLLUTION

Exposure to loud noises can damage your eardrums, and it can also affect your sleep, stress levels, blood pressure, immune system and concentration. Very loud noises can cause the body to release chemicals such as cortisol, which affects your brain and the way you think, plan and remember information. So it isn't good to do your homework with loud music in the background!

## NOISE POLLUTION IN NATURE

Animals are also affected by the loud noises that humans create. Cargo ships in the ocean emit 190 dB on average – imagine how uncomfortable that must feel for the marine creatures in the water! Noise pollution can stop animals from being able to navigate or find their way, it can interfere with their ability to find food, and it can even cause them to have fewer babies. For example, birds might get lost or change their feeding patterns while trying to avoid loud noises, which could affect their mating habits and where they can nest their eggs. That's why many wildlife organizations are campaigning for better protections against noise pollution for animals.

# WHY DO SOME SOUNDS AFFECT HOW I FEEL?

**DID YOU KNOW?**
In Spanish, the word 'grima' describes the icky feeling when you hear the sound of nails on a chalkboard or cutlery scraping on a dinner plate!

Nails on a blackboard, someone chewing loudly, teeth grinding, snoring – all of these sounds can be super annoying. Other sounds can make us feel anxious, from the ring of the school bell to the sound of the bin lorry leaving before we've put the bin out! But there are other types of noise that can relax us and even help us to sleep. So how do different noises affect us?

## I DON'T LIKE THE SOUND OF THAT . . .

Lots of people find certain sounds make them feel anxious, and it's possibly down to a part of the brain called the amygdala, which processes emotions. The amygdala is connected to the part of the brain that processes sounds, called the auditory cortex. The auditory cortex may trigger a negative response in the amygdala, and anything in the frequency range from 2,000 Hz to 5,000 Hz – the range that human hearing is the most sensitive to – may be perceived as unpleasant.

> Misophonia is a condition where certain sounds can cause someone to have a strong emotional reaction. People who have this disorder might find that particular sounds, such as chewing, heavy breathing or loud typing, cause them to feel anger, panic or disgust. People who have severe misophonia can manage it through hearing aids, therapy and a healthy daily routine.

## DANGER!

Our brains use sounds to warn us of possible threats, creating a fight-or-flight response that makes us feel like we should either run away or get ready for battle. The sounds that produce this kind of response tend to be non-linear sounds, such as animal cries, which are out of tune, extremely loud and change frequency really quickly. Our prehistoric ancestors needed to be able to react quickly to animal noises if they wanted to avoid becoming a lunchtime snack!

## COLOURFUL SOUNDS

You might have heard of white noise – a static-like sound that some people find relaxing. But did you know there are other colourful noises? Pink noise contains lower frequencies than white noise, and can sound like waves on a beach. Brown noise is more of a deep rumbling, like a heavy rainfall. These soothing background noises can help us to rest by blocking out environmental sounds that disturb our sleep, like noisy neighbours, barking dogs or police sirens.

# SOUND in SCIENCE and TECHNOLOGY

We use sound technology to help us out in our day-to-day lives, from chatting on the phone to listening to music or podcasts while we're doing chores. But did you know that sound can also be used for incredible things, such as performing brain surgery or even making objects levitate? Read on to find out more about the amazing science and technology of sound . . .

# THE FIRST TELEPHONES

It's hard to imagine life without a mobile phone, but it wasn't that long ago that we didn't have *any* phones, let alone smartphones! Before telephones, people used to send letters to keep in touch. Then, along came the telegraph, a way to transmit messages across long distances – like a very old version of sending a text message! These messages, called telegrams, were sent over a wire, and soon scientists started trying to work out how to send voices over the wire instead.

The first telephones had a transmitter and a receiver. The transmitter contained a cylinder with a covered end – a bit like a drum – attached to a needle, which was connected to a battery via a wire. The battery was connected by another wire to the receiver. If someone spoke into the transmitter, the drum-like part and the needle would vibrate like an eardrum. The vibrations were converted to an electrical current that could travel along the wire to the receiver, which translated the electrical signals into sound. The telephone allowed people to speak to each other across huge distances, and transformed the way we communicate!

**DID YOU KNOW?**

Probably the longest-distance telephone call ever was made by American president Richard Nixon in 1969, when he called Neil Armstrong and Buzz Aldrin to congratulate them on being the first people to walk on the Moon!

# STRING TELEPHONES

A string telephone works like an old wired landline telephone. You talk into a cup, sending sound-waves into it and making the bottom of the cup vibrate. The vibrations make the string vibrate, and the sound-waves travel down the string into the other cup. The other person receives the sound-waves and can hear what you are saying!

Instead of a string, modern mobile phones use radio waves and electrical signals to transfer the sound-waves through the air!

**YOU CAN MAKE A STRING TELEPHONE USING HOUSEHOLD MATERIALS. YOU WILL NEED:**

- *a needle*
- *2 paper cups*
- *a long piece of string*
- *2 paper clips*

First, use the needle to make a hole in the bottom of each paper cup. Next, thread one end of the string through the hole in one cup, then thread the other end of the string through the hole in the other cup. Tie a paper clip to one end of the string, inside the cup, then do the same with the other end of the string.

Now, hold one cup and give the other cup to a friend. Walk away from each other until the string is tight but you can still hold the cup to your mouth. Talk into your cup.

Can the other person hear what you're saying? Try grabbing the string while one of you is speaking – it will 'mute' the phone call!

**SOUND IN SCIENCE AND TECHNOLOGY**

# RADIO WAVES

Sound-waves and radio waves often get mixed up, because we listen to the radio, but the two types of wave are actually quite different. Yes, radios produce sound and sound-waves – but radio waves are part of the electromagnetic spectrum, like light. This means they travel at the speed of light, which is approximately 300,000,000 metres per second. Remember, the speed of sound in air is more like 300 metres per second!

Radio waves are transverse waves, which means the direction of movement of the wave is at right angles to the direction of movement of the vibrations. The movement is similar to moving a skipping rope quickly up and down – the waves move up and down as they travel along. Radio waves do not need a medium to travel through, so we are able to detect radio waves in a vacuum, such as outer space.

## HOW DO WE HEAR THE RADIO?

Radio stations broadcast their programmes via transmitters, which send out radio waves through an aerial. If you've ever seen a radio tower, the transmitter is usually inside the bottom of the building – and the tall tower part is actually the aerial!

All radios contain a receiver, which uses an aerial to pick up the radio waves. (You'll remember from page 18 that the first telephones had transmitters and receivers too – these do the same job in a radio broadcast, but just function a bit differently!) If you change the tuning on a radio, it changes what frequency of radio wave will be picked up, allowing you to select which show you want to listen to. The radio converts the radio waves into mechanical vibrations via the speaker, which in turn creates movement in the air in front of it. The vibrations in the air are the sound-waves that are picked up by your ear.

The reason we can hear radio waves when we can't hear other parts of the electromagnetic spectrum, such as light, is because the frequency of radio waves is within the hearing range of humans. A radio wave can be converted into a sound-wave with the same frequency. So, a radio transmission uses both sound-waves and radio waves to send songs and voices around the world!

## DID YOU KNOW?

Since radio waves travel so much faster than soundwaves, someone listening to a concert on the radio may hear the music a fraction of a second sooner than the people at the back of the concert hall!

SOUND IN SCIENCE AND TECHNOLOGY

# INFRASOUND – MAKING YOU SHIVER

You've already learned about how some sounds might make you feel funny, but infrasound – sound that is at a frequency too low for humans to hear – can send shivers down your spine, almost like you've seen a ghost!

Since infrasound is very low frequency, it means that we can still sense something is happening, even though we can't hear it – and that can make us feel uneasy, anxious or sad. Nowadays, lots of human-built machines make infrasound. Wind farms are one example, as are certain types of transport. This means we are more exposed to infrasound today than we used to be, and scientists don't know for certain how this might affect the human body. However, infrasound is also a part of the natural world. It's produced by earthquakes and storms, and elephants can even use it to communicate across long distances!

## EASY BREATHING

Low-frequency sound-waves that are just above the range of infrasound can help people with breathing difficulties. The Lung Flute, created by engineer Sandy Hawkins, is a small device with a tube and mouthpiece. A person blows into the mouthpiece, and this causes vibrations to travel into their lungs. This can help to remove mucus and dirt trapped in the lungs, and help the person to breathe more easily.

## ULTRASOUND – CLEANING AND BABIES

At the other end of the sound spectrum is ultrasound – very high-frequency sound-waves. Ultrasound waves can be used to take pictures of things inside the body. For instance, when people are pregnant, they can have an ultrasound scan to see what their baby looks like! The sound-waves are at a frequency that's too high for humans to hear, but they can pass through the body without causing harm. The waves bounce and reflect off parts of the body, and the echoes are turned into a moving image using a computer and a monitor.

Ultrasound can also be used for cleaning jewellery, surgical instruments and glass lenses. Most cleaners use sound at a frequency between 35 kHz and 45 kHz, which releases energy and creates bubbles that burst, causing microscopic shock waves that break up and scatter any dirt stuck on the surface! Can you imagine having an 'ultrasonic bath' at bedtime? You'd be clean in no time – but the force of those bubbles might sting a little!

## BRAIN SURGERY

Researchers are working on a new treatment that uses ultrasound to target and destroy brain tumours. A brain surgeon uses magnetic resonance imaging (MRI) technology to see inside the brain and locate the tumour, then directs a beam of high-frequency sound into the skull. The beam of ultrasound produces heat, which works to destroy the tumour. The person's skull must be cooled by chilled water at the same time to stop their brain from overheating. It sounds scary, but it could be a safe and effective way to treat cancer patients without causing damage to the skull.

SOUND IN SCIENCE AND TECHNOLOGY

# The Power of Sound

## A SOURCE OF ENERGY

You might be surprised to learn that sound can be used to heat our homes! This is very useful for people who live in countries where the electricity supply is limited. A team of researchers has created a wood-burning stove that focuses excess heat into a thermo-acoustic engine, which causes the air trapped inside it to vibrate. And, as we know, vibrations equal sound! A device called an alternator then changes the sound into electricity. After three hours of burning, the stove creates enough electricity to power a home for the night!

## TAKING A TEMPERATURE

When you're not feeling well, you might reach for a thermometer to take your temperature. Some thermometers work using a type of light called infrared, but scientists have also created a thermometer that uses sound! These acoustic thermometers are very accurate, so can be used in extreme conditions – such as in a nuclear reactor, where the temperature needs to be monitored very closely to avoid dangerous overheating.

The thermometer is made from a ceramic tube with a speaker at one end and a microphone at the other. Sound-waves travel from one end to the other, and the thermometer measures the time it takes for the waves to get across the ceramic tube. Remember, the speed of sound changes with temperature – so, the faster the sound travels, the warmer the air is!

## ACOUSTIC LEVITATION

Levitation is when things float above the ground. This can be done with magnets, but it's also possible to make objects levitate using sound! To do this, scientists use speakers that make sounds at higher frequencies than humans can hear. These speakers form a pattern of sounds that surround the object. All the sound-waves added together create a combined force that is strong enough to hold objects in mid-air!

Scientists have done this with small insects, cells, and even fish! And acoustic levitation has been used for experiments in space, too, as it can be a way to control liquids in microgravity environments.

Gravity is a force that attracts objects together. The more mass an object has, or the more matter they contain, the greater the effect of gravity will be. Earth's gravity pulls everything on its surface down towards its centre. It's the reason why things fall down when we drop them. Gravity gets weaker the further away you are from an object – so in space, the further away you travel from a planet, the weaker its force of gravity will be. This is what we call microgravity: when the effect of gravity is very small.

## DID YOU KNOW?

There is an app that uses sound to blow out candles! It uses the sound speaker in your phone in a clever way: by emitting a sound at a certain frequency, the speaker creates vibrations in the air that are strong enough to move air molecules away from the flame. This disrupts the flow of oxygen, which makes the fire go out, extinguishing the candle.

**SOUND IN SCIENCE AND TECHNOLOGY**

# SOUND in MUSIC and PERFORMANCE

One of the most joyful ways to create sound is to make music! From thigh-slapping and clicking our tongues to playing instruments and singing, humans have used music to communicate and connect with each other for as long as we've been on Earth. We use music to express all kinds of emotions, to tell stories and to celebrate life's big moments. So, get ready for a symphony of sound as we explore how music is made, where it comes from and why it makes us feel good.

# A MUSICAL TIMELINE

A lot of our knowledge about ancient music is based on ancient instruments (or objects that we *think* were instruments) found by archaeologists. And because early music wasn't written down, much of what we know comes from the rituals and ceremonies of Indigenous people, which have been handed down through generations. Here are some of the musical discoveries that we do know about . . .

← TRUMPET

### PREHISTORIC TIMES
The first musical instruments were probably basic drums made from rocks or animal skins, with sticks used as drumsticks. We don't know a lot about the earliest instruments, as they would have been made from natural materials that weathered away over time.

### 1500 BCE (AROUND 3,500 YEARS AGO)
Trumpets have been around for thousands of years – ever since humans discovered they could make sounds by blowing into hollow objects like conch shells! It's thought humans started crafting trumpets from wood and metal around 1500 BCE.

### 3000 BCE (AROUND 5,000 YEARS AGO)
Ancient Egyptian paintings of harps exist that date from around 3000 BCE. The lyre – which is similar to the harp, but has two upright arms instead of a single bow – is thought to have been invented in Iran in 3200 BCE.

### 50,000 YEARS AGO
The oldest flute is thought to be around 50,000 years old, and was discovered in Slovenia. It was carved from the bone of a cave bear.

LYRE →

### 1400 BCE (AROUND 3,400 YEARS AGO)

A Sumerian hymn unearthed in the 1950s is the oldest sheet music we've got! It looks very different to the sheet music we recognize today, as it's written in cuneiform – a type of writing a bit like hieroglyphics. The music was etched on to clay tablets, and is thought to be about 3,400 years old.

### 1000 BCE (AROUND 3,000 YEARS AGO)

The first lamellophones – instruments made from a board base with different-sized prongs attached – started to appear about 3,000 years ago. Bamboo and metal mbiras, or 'thumb pianos', date back at least this far, although the materials used to make them has changed a lot. The tines, or prongs, were first made from bamboo, then metal, and nowadays you can find modern lamellophones made from recycled tin cans and rubbish!

**DID YOU KNOW?**
The ancient Chinese were the first people to categorize music by the material that the instrument was made with. They had eight categories: wood, stone, metal, clay, gourd, animal hide, bamboo and silk.

### 1500S (500 YEARS AGO)

The violin was invented in sixteenth-century Italy, though it's thought to have its origins in much older stringed instruments, such as the Arabian rabāb, a type of fiddle popular in the middle ages.

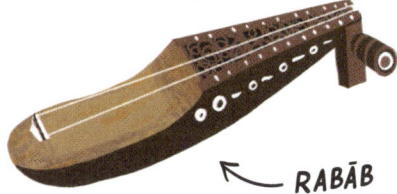

← RABĀB

### 1600S TO 1900S (400-100 YEARS AGO)

Pianos were invented in Italy in the late 1600s or early 1700s, but became more popular in Europe and worldwide between the 1750s and 1900s.

### TODAY

The twentieth century saw the invention of electronic instruments, such as synthesizers, and the birth of digital music. Nowadays computers have revolutionized how we use instruments and make music!

← MBIRAS

**SOUND IN MUSIC AND PERFORMANCE**

# HOW DO MUSICAL INSTRUMENTS WORK?

All musical instruments – whether stringed, brass, woodwind or percussion – create sound in the same way as everything else: vibrations!

## STRINGED INSTRUMENTS

In stringed instruments, such as violins, cellos or guitars, the sounds are created by plucking strings, rubbing a bow on strings or hitting strings. As the strings vibrate, so does the air around them, creating the sound-waves that are picked up by our ears.

Most stringed instruments also have a sound box attached to them to make the sound louder. The vibrations of the strings are picked up by the bridge of the instrument, which usually connects the strings to the sound box. The vibrations are transferred from the bridge across to the sound box, and as the sound box vibrates it amplifies the sound. You can change the note on a stringed instrument by changing the length, weight or tightness of the strings. Shorter, lighter, tighter strings make the highest-pitched notes.

### DID YOU KNOW?

Pianos are a stringed instrument! If you press down on a note, a hammer hits a string inside the piano, causing the vibrations and the sounds.

**SOUND IN MUSIC AND PERFORMANCE**

### DID YOU KNOW?

Astronauts are allowed to take one item of their choosing into space – and some choose musical instruments. So far there has been a flute, a saxophone, a keyboard and even a didgeridoo in space!

## BRASS AND WOODWIND INSTRUMENTS

Wind instruments fall into two groups: brass and woodwind. The main difference is what they're made of (though there are other differences, too), and they include instruments such as trumpets and saxophones. Another key difference is the direction the music travels from the instrument. For a woodwind instrument the sound will be the same whether you stand in front of the musician or behind them, but for a brass instrument the music is *directional*, which means it sounds louder if you're in front of the musician.

For a trumpet, which is brass, the vibrations are created by pressing the lips up to the mouthpiece and blowing. For a saxophone, which is woodwind, the lips vibrate on a piece of wood called a reed. In both, the rest of the instrument amplifies the sound.

## PERCUSSION INSTRUMENTS

Percussion instruments, such as drums, rattles and cymbals, are played by hitting, shaking, rubbing, plucking or scraping to produce vibrations. Drums, for example, have a tightly stretched skin that vibrates when you hit it with a stick or your hand.

# HOW DOES SINGING WORK?

The human voice is a type of instrument – without it, we couldn't use noises and language to communicate, and nor could we sing! In our throats we have a larynx, or voice box. The larynx stops food from going down the wrong way, allows air to get to your lungs and produces sound.

In your larynx, you have two vocal cords, which are two flexible, bendy bands of muscle. When you breathe, air passes across the vocal cords, causing them to move together and apart again, creating vibrations – and sound! Different sounds are produced depending on how big or small the gap is between the vocal cords. To keep your larynx healthy, you should avoid screaming at high-pitched levels, make sure to drink lots of water and rest your throat if it has been sore.

## SMASHING WORK!

Perhaps you've seen films where someone sings a high note and cracks a glass? This can actually happen if the singer hits a note that is at the same frequency as the natural resonance of the glass. All objects, including glass, are made up of particles that vibrate at a certain frequency. So, if you strike a glass, the note you hear will have the frequency of these natural vibrations. If you sing a note that has the same frequency, it causes the particles to vibrate harder – so the glass may smash. The sound needs to be very loud in order for this to work, but one professional rock singer did manage to crack a glass with a high note of 105 dB!

## SOUND-WAVE ART

Did you know that you can turn your voice into a piece of artwork? Your voice is a bit like your fingerprint – totally unique. Every sound, and every voice, has its own unique wave pattern. With technology, you can record a sound, then turn it into a visualization that can be printed on to a poster, turned into a piece of clothing or worn as jewellery. Some visual artists have even raised money for charity by turning famous songs into sound-wave art, then selling the art pieces. And they can raise even more money if the musician signs it!

SOUND IN MUSIC AND PERFORMANCE

# WHY DOES MUSIC MAKE US FEEL GOOD?

Have you ever noticed how a grown-up can hear a song from a long time ago and suddenly start singing along to every single word? How do they remember all those lyrics, when they can't even remember what's on their shopping list?

Music can create lots of powerful emotions in all of us. It can bring back old memories, create feelings of joy or sadness, or make us want to dance. It is such an important part of our lives, even if we don't realize it! But why does music make us feel the way it does?

## A DOPAMINE HIT

Listening to music causes blood to travel to the area of the brain that creates memories and generates emotions. This part of the brain releases dopamine, a chemical messenger that makes us feel joy and pleasure. Every time you hear a particular song, this chemical trigger happens and dopamine is released – so, eventually, even if you just hear the start of the song your brain makes you feel happy.

## MUSIC AND MEMORY

The brain has to work hard to understand music, because there are so many different layers to it, including the pitch, rhythm and lyrics. This creates a lot of mental work for your brain – similar to when you're learning to read or memorizing your times tables – and this effort engages your memory and makes it stronger.

Memory and emotions are closely linked, so the memory of a song can remind you of how you were feeling at the time that you first heard it. This is why grown-ups might remember a song from when they were young and suddenly feel like their teenage selves again – and still remember all the words!

**DID YOU KNOW?**

After Beethoven lost his hearing, he sawed the legs off his piano so that when he played it on the floor he could feel the vibrations made by the music!

Listening to music has been shown to have a positive effect on people with dementia, a condition that causes memory loss. Hearing a particular song can sometimes help people with this illness to remember their past. A 90-year-old former ballerina with Alzheimer's (the most common form of dementia) called Marta C. Gonzalez was still able to remember the dance moves from one of her performances as soon as she heard the song played again!

# HOW DO WE PLAY and RECORD MUSIC?

Have you ever wondered how the music you listen to was recorded? Or how thousands of songs can be stored on your phone? Since the first song was recorded in 1860, we've invented lots of different ways to play and record music. So, let's take a look at how they work...

## EARLY SOUND RECORDING

In the 1850s, a French bookseller called Édouard-Léon Scott de Martinville invented a device called a phonautograph that recorded sound. It worked a bit like a human ear, focusing sound on to one spot, vibrating a diaphragm (a very thin sheet of material like an eardrum), and making a pen move and write the sounds down in ink. This device wasn't made to play sounds back to listeners – but it did inspire the birth of sound recording!

## GROOVY GRAMOPHONES

In 1887, a German-American inventor called Emile Berliner came up with the gramophone, a device that used records to play back music. A record is a flat, circular disc with a pattern of grooves etched on its surface that relate to the patterns in a piece of music. Berliner's records were originally made from celluloid (a type of plastic), and later from hard rubber.

The gramophone reads the sound pattern by running a needle over the grooves in the record. The needle is attached to a diaphragm, which is attached to a horn. You turn a handle on the base of the machine, which spins the record. As the needle vibrates up and down, it makes the diaphragm vibrate too, creating sound. The horn amplifies the sound, sending the music out into the room.

By the 1890s, many people were using gramophones, and they soon became the most popular listening device.

## PUT YOUR RECORDS ON

In the 1950s, gramophones were replaced by record players, which also used flat discs, but these ones were made from a material called vinyl – and that's where vinyl records get their name from! Instead of a handle, record players have a turntable to spin the record, and they use electricity to send signals to an amplifier and a speaker to create music.

## ROLL THE TAPE

Magnetic tapes are another way of recording music that first became popular in the 1930s. A cassette tape contains a piece of plastic tape covered in magnetic material. When it's connected to a recording device, the special magnetic tape inside the cassette is able to capture the sound patterns in a piece of music – a bit like the grooves in a vinyl record.

## THE RISE OF DIGITAL MUSIC

Digital recording devices started to appear in the 1960s and 1970s, and compact discs (CDs) first become available in 1982. CDs are a bit like digital records: they also read sound patterns, but the information is pressed into the disc using a laser that creates grooves called pits.

Digital recording methods work by turning sounds into long strings of numbers, which can be read by different devices, such as a smartphone. This digital information can be read by computers in the same way that someone might read a piece of sheet music!

# WHAT ARE ACOUSTICS?

Sometimes, you might struggle to hear what your teacher is saying when you're sitting in a big school hall for assembly. Or maybe you've wondered how a singer can fill a whole theatre with just their voice?

Well, it's all to do with acoustics – a branch of science that deals with sound, including how it is produced, controlled, carried and heard, and how it affects objects. The way sound travels indoors, for instance, depends on what is in the room, how big the room is, and the materials that the furniture in the room is made from. All of these things make up the acoustics of the room. Good acoustics allow us to hear sounds clearly, while bad acoustics can muffle sound or produce lots of background noise.

One effect of bad acoustics is that there can be too much reverberation, which is when sounds bounce between reflective surfaces in an indoor space, creating a kind of super echo! Some reverberation can be good, as it amplifies the sound, but too much can mean it becomes difficult to hear clearly.

Hard surfaces reflect sound, causing reverberations. Soft surfaces, such as a thick carpet, absorb sound – when the sound-wave travels into the soft material, the energy of the sound-wave is transformed into something else, such as heat energy, which reduces the sound.

## HARD TO HEAR AT HARVARD

In the late 1800s, students at Harvard University in the United States were struggling to hear their lectures because the acoustics in the lecture hall were so bad. Whenever a lecturer was speaking, their voice reverberated so much the lecture sounded like nonsense!

A physics professor decided to investigate the problem, and found that there was a link between the reverberations and the size and shape of the room, as well how many people were in it and how absorbent the conditions were. When the professor added sound-absorbing material to the walls of the lecture theatre, it reduced the reverberation – and the lectures made sense again!

## WHY DOES MY SINGING SOUND BETTER IN THE SHOWER?

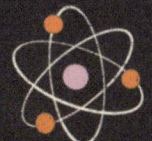

Perhaps you've noticed how belting out your favourite song in the shower sounds way better than usual? Well, this isn't because you're using the shower head as a microphone! Rather, it's because the hard surfaces inside the shower reflect the sound, causing echoes and reverberations. This amplifies the sound, making your singing louder and stronger. These noises are all made split seconds behind one another, then combined in your ear. This 'smears' out the sound, making it seem more in tune, richer and deeper – and making you think you sound like the next big singing superstar!

# HOW DOES SOUND TRAVEL IN A CONCERT HALL?

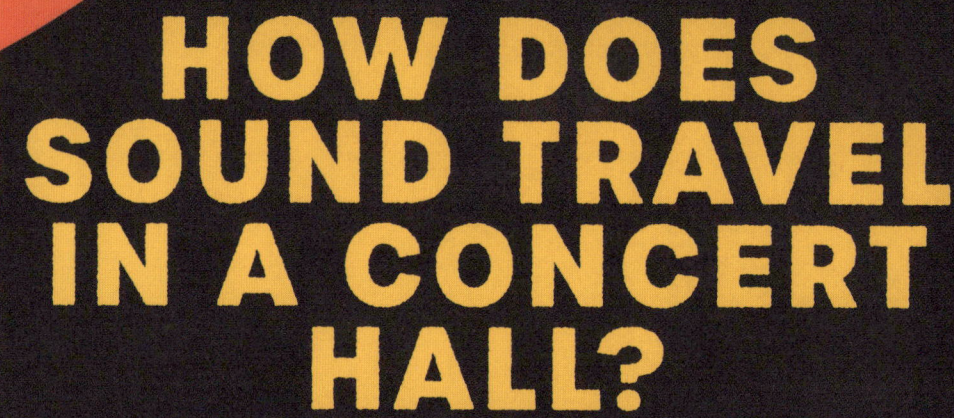

Concert halls are cleverly designed to enrich the music that you hear, so that you'll feel as though you're sitting in the middle of the orchestra even if you're seated right at the back!

## DID YOU KNOW?

The famous lecture theatre in the Royal Institution in London, in the United Kingdom, is specially shaped so that it has the perfect acoustics. The room is round and deep with a dome on top, and if you stand in the middle of the lecture-theatre floor you can be heard clearly by everyone – without a microphone!

### HERE ARE THE SECRETS TO CREATING THE BEST SOUND:

- **A shoebox-shaped hall.** Engineers experimented with many different-shaped rooms and found that a rectangular-shaped concert hall is best!

- **Hard and rough surfaces** to reflect unwanted noise away from the audience, so they can focus on the music.

- **Acoustic panels.** These are tiles made of a material that absorbs sound and reduces echoes and reverberation. Acoustic panels stop sound from escaping into the outside world – so the neighbours don't get annoyed!

- **A layer of air between the inside and outside walls** to stop sound from the outside seeping in. Some concert halls are even built on springs, which absorb vibrations from traffic or trains.

## WHISPERS ALONG A WALL

Whispering galleries are another fascinating example of how acoustics can be changed by the shape of a building. If you sit in a circular whispering gallery and your friend is sitting on the opposite side, whispering to someone else, you can hear the words as clearly as if they were right next to you! It might seem like magic, but there is science behind this.

Whispers, shouts and singing are all sound-waves created by your larynx vibrating. Because a whisper is so quiet, it is low-pitched and has a low amplitude, meaning that the sound-wave is small and quite flat. The sound-waves bounce around in the dome and along the curved, hard wall. The sound-waves are able to bounce and reflect horizontally along the wall, until they are picked up by someone listening. This works better with whispers, because the angle of reflection is very small, allowing the whisper to bounce round many times. It's a bit like skimming flat pebbles on the surface of a lake. If you whisper *at* the wall, instead of *along* it, it doesn't work so well, in the same way that a flat pebble won't skim if you throw it *into* the water.

# SOUND in the ANIMAL KINGDOM

Animals use sounds for many different reasons – to warn each other of danger, when looking for a mate and to effectively hunt for prey. Different animals (and that includes humans!) make noise and hear sounds in different ways, but communication is something we all have in common – whether it's speaking English, barking or purring! Read on to discover some amazing animal orchestras . . .

# ANIMAL ORCHESTRAS

Did you know that some animals have their own built-in musical instruments? And it's not just bigger beasts that can make loud noises – even the smallest creatures can create a cacophony of sound!

## A TINY VIOLIN

Perhaps you've heard crickets chirping outside in the summer months. Did you know that they create this sound by playing their bodies like a güiro, the wooden percussion instrument with ridges in it that you rub a stick along?

To sing its song, the male cricket raises its wings one above the other, and rubs them together. It rubs the sharp edge, called a scraper, on the top of one wing against the wrinkly bit on the underside of the other wing, called a file. This causes vibrations, which we hear as a chirping sound!

And crickets chirp more often when the temperature rises. One theory says that you can tell the air temperature by counting how many chirps there are in fifteen seconds, then add thirty-seven, which gives you the temperature in degrees Fahrenheit!

## HOWLING MONKEYS

Howler monkeys have a hollow bone in their throat that amplifies their howls, making them the loudest monkeys on the planet! They howl to communicate with other howler monkeys, and to make sure rivals know to stay away. They make lots of noise in the morning and evening, and their screams can be heard for miles. They also like to make a din during a rainstorm. Maybe they don't like getting wet!

### DID YOU KNOW?

Crickets have ears on their knees! Their ears work in a similar way to human ears, with an eardrum and a tube like a cochlea, but they are located just below the knees of the front legs.

## A TREMENDOUS TRUMPET

If you hear a rumble in the jungle, it could be an elephant playing its 'trumpet'! Elephants can create a trumpet-like sound by forcing air down their trunks. It's a bit like when we blow raspberries by forcing air out of our closed lips.

Elephants can also make very low rumbling noises by pushing air through their vocal cords. Their vocal cords are much longer than human ones – ours are around 2 centimetres long, while an elephant's can be up to 10 centimetres! This means that they can make vibrations at frequencies that are too low for humans to hear. Since the frequency is so low, the rumbling sounds have very long wavelengths, so the sounds can travel further. Elephants can use these rumbles to communicate with other elephants up to 10 kilometres away!

SOUND IN THE ANIMAL KINGDOM

# DO ANIMALS SOUND DIFFERENT IN OTHER COUNTRIES?

If you speak English, you might think that cows 'moo', sheep 'baa' and frogs 'ribbit'. But if you asked someone from a country that speaks a different language, they might use a different word altogether! For example:

Chinese dogs say 'wāng'

In Arabic, horses 'saheel' and in Lithuanian a horse says 'yii-gaga'!

There are lots of reasons why different languages use different sounds to describe animal noises. It could be to do with how the language is structured, and which sounds are most commonly used by native speakers. And some languages might not have words for certain animal sounds because those animals don't live in the countries where they are spoken.

Some words for animal sounds are onomatopoeic, which means they sound like the noise of the word they describe – such as 'buzz' or 'hiss'! The onomatopoeic words for animal sounds tend to sound similar across different languages – wolf howls are 'awooooo' in English, 'oooooou' in Dutch and 'huuuuuuu' in Italian!

## RIBBIT, RIBBIT . . .

If you've listened to a frog, you might have noticed that their sound is more like a croak than a ribbit. In fact, it's only in the United Kingdom and the United States that we call a frog's noise a ribbit. This is thought to be because Hollywood film makers used the noise of the Pacific tree frog as a sound effect in old movies, and that particular species of frog does make a ribbiting noise. The people who watched those films heard the ribbiting background noises, and the sound stuck!

Spanish roosters say 'quiquiriquí' and Chinese ones say 'gu gu gu'!

In French, pigs 'groin' and a horse says 'hiii' and Hungarian pigs go 'röf'

SOUND IN THE ANIMAL KINGDOM

# WHY DO DOGS BARK BUT WOLVES HOWL?

**DID YOU KNOW?**
Wolves really do 'wolf down' their dinner – they can eat up to 9 kg of food in one go!

Can you make a howling sound? What about a barking noise? Chances are you said 'awooo' first, then 'woof'! But, as you might already know, modern dogs are actually descended from wolves – so why have they ended up sounding different?

**DID YOU KNOW?**
The first dog to travel to space was a Russian stray named Laika, which means 'barker' – she was given the name after she was heard barking on a radio show!

**SOUND IN THE ANIMAL KINGDOM**

**DID YOU KNOW?**
Dogs aren't the only animals that bark. Deer, monkeys and even birds bark, too. Dogs are just more famous for it!

Mammals, including wolves, howl by pushing air through their vocal cords. Their vocal cords vibrate in different ways to make howls, barks and other noises, too. Wolves can make all sorts of noises, and they use them in different ways to communicate different things. Howling is particularly useful for animals that live in packs, like wolves do, as it is a good way to communicate over several kilometres! Wolves howl to locate the other members of their pack and bring them back together again. And, sometimes, a wolf pack might howl all together in a chorus!

The reason dogs tend to bark instead of howl is because they've been trained to do so over thousands of years of living with humans. Over time, dogs have become domesticated, which means they have adapted to live with humans instead of in the wild. Wild dogs make natural noises like whining and squealing, but pet dogs have been bred for specific reasons, and that has altered how noisy they are. For instance, dogs bark when they are under attack, and humans used to breed dogs to fight, hunt and guard – which meant that dogs became more used to barking. By comparison, wolves and wild dogs run away if they feel under attack, so don't need to bark so much. Wolves *can* bark, they just don't need to. And pet dogs don't live in packs, so they don't really need to howl, either!

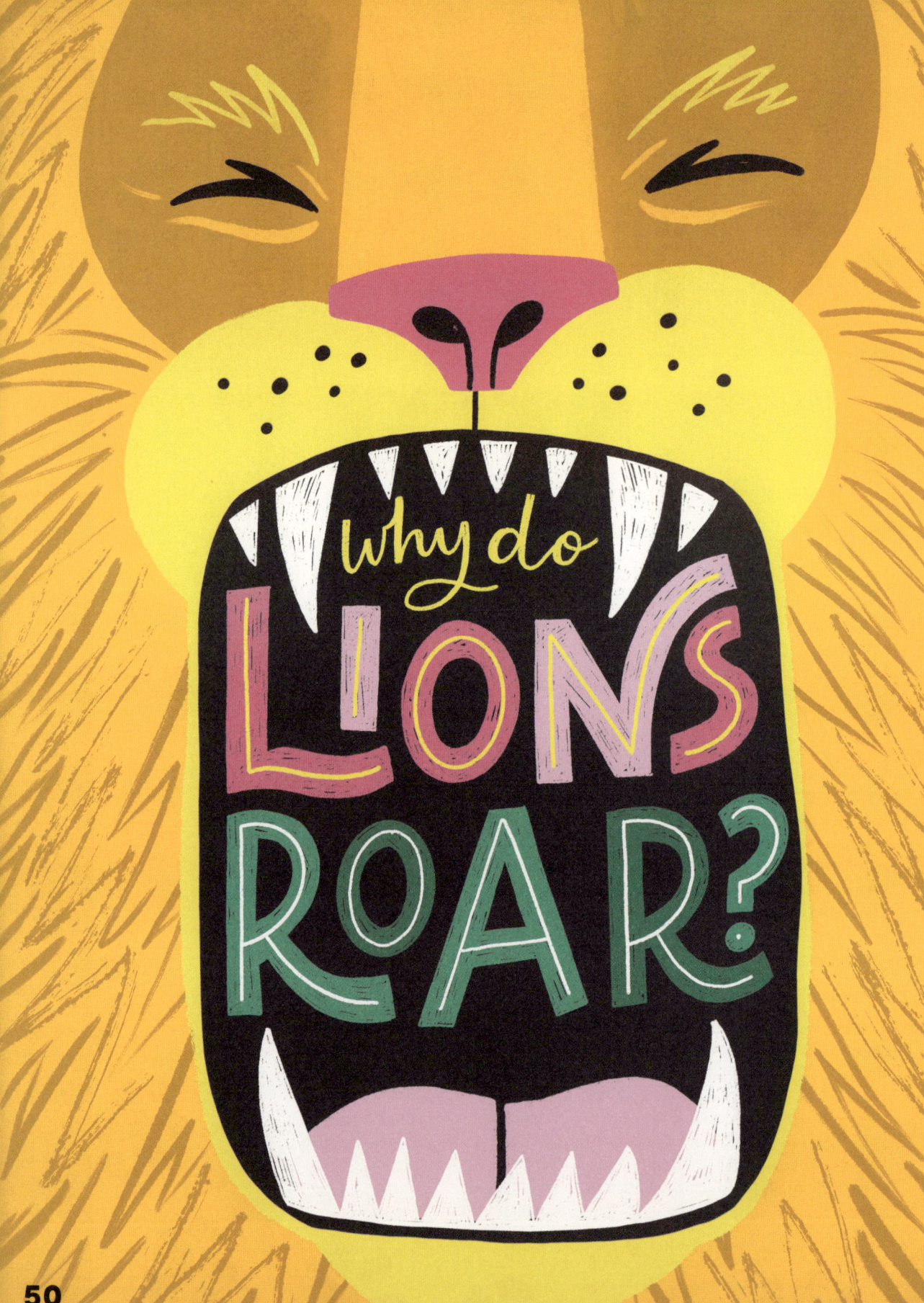

Lions roar to show other lions how powerful they are – they're letting them know who's boss! In the wild, lions are very social, and live in prides made of a small number of male lions and up to twelve female lions and their young. The male lions roar to scare away intruders, communicate with other lions and to attract a mate.

## WHY DO CATS PURR?

You might think that cats purr because they're happy and content, right? Actually, there are lots of different reasons why cats purr, and not all cats do it for the same ones! Some cats purr when they are nervous or frightened. Others purr when they are being fed – a leftover trait from when they were kittens and purred so that their mum could find them and feed them. And cats sometimes purr when investigating new territories, like a cardboard box or the back of your wardrobe!

How cats purr is actually still a bit of a mystery. We know that cats have pads of tissue in their vocal cords, which allow the vocal cords to vibrate more slowly and produce a low-frequency sound. But we still don't know whether cats deliberately use their muscles to control purring, or whether it's an automatic response from the brain. Some scientists think it may be both!

Purring is also thought to help cats to heal and strengthen their bones and joints! Some people believe that the vibrations from the purring can stimulate cats' bones and tissue to grow harder and stronger. Magic!

Lions have the loudest roar of all the big cats. The power and tone of a lion's roar helps it to distinguish itself from other lions, so everyone knows who is in charge. And, since its roars are so loud – up to 114 dB – lions can 'shout' at their friends and foes up to 8 kilometres away!

There are only four big cats that can roar: lions, tigers, leopards and jaguars. Pumas, cheetahs and other cats can only purr! The biggest cats have larger larynxes with more folds, which allow for bigger vibrations. The bones around the larynx are able to stretch further than in other cats and produce a deep, rumbling ROAR!

SOUND IN THE ANIMAL KINGDOM

# ARE MICE REALLY THAT QUIET?

You may have heard the saying 'as quiet as a mouse', but if you've ever met a mouse you'll know that they can be very noisy indeed! Mice squeak in lots of different ways to express themselves. If you listen closely to a mouse, its sounds will make up a song that changes in pitch and frequency depending on whether it feels safe, hungry or happy!

Squeaky mice might be looking for friends nearby, or telling them something. If they make loud noises, they may have found food – and they are most active on their hunt for something to eat at sunset or sunrise. This is because mice are nocturnal creatures, which means they tend to be awake at night and sleep during the day. And, if their squeaks are faster and closer together, they may be in danger. (Watch out for that cat!)

Female mice respond more to male mice when mating if the male mice produce ultrasonic vocalizations. Ultrasonic sounds are so high-pitched that humans are unable to hear them, and vocalizations are sounds that animals (including humans) make with their vocal cords. The male mice make these ultrasonic vocalizations by pushing air out of their bodies really fast, which gives them an incredibly high-pitched squeak. And it's these super-high squeaks that seem to get the most attention from the female mice. I guess if we heard a noise like that, it would get our attention, too!

SOUND IN THE ANIMAL KINGDOM

# CAN CHIMPANZEES TALK TO EACH OTHER?

Chimpanzees might not use a spoken language, but we think they use both vocal and visual means of communication, just like humans do. Humans can communicate using sign language, words and actions to deliberately send messages to other humans. Chimps and other apes can also use deliberate forms of communication – they might use hand signs or specific noises to ask to be groomed, to move up and make space, or for a piggyback!

Scientists think that some of the sounds chimps make might not have specific meanings, but they can still make themselves understood. It's a bit like when a baby screams because their bath water is too hot. The baby isn't actually saying, 'This is too hot', but their parent or carer understands why they are screaming.

## DID YOU KNOW?

When we speak face to face, between 70 and 90 per cent of what we say comes from non-verbal communication – our body language and facial expressions – and the rest is from communicating verbally, or talking.

# SOUND on the EARTH

You might think that the ground beneath our feet is completely silent, but did you know that the Earth actually hums? Our planet has a low-frequency background noise of between 2 and 7 millihertz (mHz) – that's about 10,000 times lower than humans can hear! Scientists think these vibrations are caused by changes in the atmosphere and ocean, such as storms and crashing waves, which cause the sea-floor to shake back and forth.

As well as this background noise, sounds in the Earth can range from rumbling earthquakes to creaking ice and singing mountains. Let's go underground to find out more about Earth's natural music . . .

# WHAT ARE EARTHQUAKES?

Earthquakes occur when two tectonic plates, or large pieces of the Earth's crust, slip or rub past each other. This causes shock waves and vibrations that shake the Earth's surface. Earthquakes often happen at the edges of the plates, which are called fault lines, where they can move over each other or get stuck. Pressure builds up until the plates shift, and this can create an earthquake.

The shock waves caused by an earthquake are called seismic waves, and they can move through the Earth at twenty times the speed of sound in air! Seismic waves are waves of sound energy that travel through the Earth as vibrations. They can result from earthquakes, volcanic eruptions, landslides and human-made explosions, such as during fracking, which involves drilling into the Earth to extract oil or gas.

Seismic waves are measured on a scale called the Moment Magnitude Scale (MMS). The larger the number, the larger the earthquake. A magnitude 4 earthquake might just feel like a lorry passing by your house, while a magnitude 8 quake could cause cracks in the Earth and make buildings and bridges fall down.

## SHOCK WAVES

There are three different types of seismic wave created by an earthquake: primary (P) waves, secondary (S) waves and surface waves. P waves travel fast and are longitudinal, meaning they contract and expand, moving in a motion just like sound-waves. S waves are transverse and move more slowly than P waves, so they strike seconds later. Both P waves and S waves travel deep underground, while surface waves travel along the Earth's surface – which is why these are the ones that cause most damage to buildings and structures.

## LISTENING TO EARTHQUAKES

We can't hear earthquakes because the frequency of the seismic waves is below the range of human hearing. But, since P waves behave like sound-waves, geophysicists (a scientist who studies the physics of the Earth) *can* record them and translate them into sounds they can actually listen to. They use these sounds to work out where quakes come from, and where they are going.

The sounds of an earthquake can be recorded and heard up to seven weeks after it hits as aftershocks – smaller earthquakes that happen after the main quake.

### DID YOU KNOW?

The largest ever earthquake recorded was 9.5 on the MMS scale, and took place in Chile in 1960.

## MARSQUAKES

Mars has quakes, too – but they're called *marsquakes!* A spacecraft called the *InSight* lander has been used to measure these quakes. One of the biggest ever recorded was magnitude 5, and so far there have been more than 1,300 marsquakes recorded by the mission. We can use marsquake data to learn more about what is going on under the surface of Mars, why the quakes happen and how the planet formed about 5 billion years ago.

SOUND ON THE EARTH

# EXPLORING THE EARTH

By listening to seismic waves, scientists can work out what is beneath the surface of the Earth! This process is called a seismic survey and it's used to explore the different layers of Earth's crust.

First, a large plate is pressed against the ground, using a special truck. The plate sends out a sound pulse, which travels through the Earth. As the sound pulse meets different layers in the Earth, it gets reflected back to the truck and captured by recording devices. Scientists can use the reflections to work out the type of rock and how deep it goes.

## LIFE UNDERGROUND

It's not just humans who can use vibrations to explore underground. Some animals, including types of moles, amphibians and lizards, have enlarged inner-ear bones or oversized organs in their ears so that they can pick up more vibrations while underground, helping them to navigate.

And there are other underground animals with some truly amazing adaptations – for instance, the naked mole-rat has very fine hair all over its body that it uses to feel for vibrations in the soil, and the star-nosed mole has special tentacles on its nose that are super-sensitive to even the slightest movement!

## WORM-CHARMING

If you stand on damp grass and stomp your feet gently and lightly in a rhythmic pattern, you might suddenly be surrounded by earthworms! Worms have no eyes, but they can feel the vibrations that your feet make. They think the trembling is a mole coming to eat them, so they scurry away, up to the surface. No one knows why they go upwards – the surface isn't particularly safe for them either, as they could just as easily be eaten by a bird!

SOUND ON THE EARTH

# SINGING MOUNTAINS

> **DID YOU KNOW?**
> Research has shown that the Matterhorn, a mountain in Switzerland, 'sings' at a frequency of about 0.43 Hz!

When you look at a mountain, it doesn't appear to move – right? Well, you might be surprised to learn that mountains *do* move, but the vibrations are just too small for humans to see.

Mountains vibrate becase of seismic energy in the Earth beneath them, which comes from earthquakes, movement in the ocean, and human activity such as drilling. These vibrations can be measured using a device called a seismometer, and the measurements can then be turned into sound-waves and amplified so that humans can hear them. The vibrations are stronger at the summit of a mountain, because the top of a mountain can move more freely than the base, like a tree swaying in the wind.

Listening to the songs of mountains could be quite important: it could be used to measure how stable slopes are and the possibility of earthquakes, landslides and rockfalls at mountains that are popular tourist destinations. But these 'singing' mountains wouldn't make a very good choir – most only vibrate in one or two frequencies, so they could only hum a couple of notes!

## RAINBOW BRIDGE

There is an arch of sandstone in Utah, in the United States, called the Rainbow Bridge, because it is shaped like a rainbow. When the bridge is affected by other sounds (such as the waves on a lake) or geological activity (such as earthquakes), it rocks very slightly and vibrates. Scientists can measure these vibrations to learn more about the stability of the structure, and work out how long the arch might last for. Tourists to the area have even reported hearing a low humming noise!

Have you ever stood next to a frozen pond in winter and heard it make strange creaking noises? This happens naturally, as the ice is affected by temperature changes. These sounds can also help to warn us of ice that isn't safe to stand on.

Temperature changes cause ice to move across itself and shift around in water. The ice expands and contracts as the temperature rises and falls, and this growing and shrinking of ice is what creates the sounds we hear. The sounds are more obvious at times of the day when temperatures change suddenly – such as when the Sun sets, or when the Sun shines directly on the ice. The surface of the ice acts like a giant eardrum, vibrating to create sound!

Thicker ice makes less sound, as it isn't able to move and vibrate as much. If the noise of the ice is particularly high-pitched, this means it is very thin and probably not safe to walk on. If ice is covered in snow it won't make as much noise, because the snow absorbs the sound and muffles it. But, if ice is clear and smooth, the sounds can travel further, because the super-smooth surface allows sounds to bounce and reflect along it.

## SKATING AND SINGING ON ICE

If you skate on clear ice, you can make the ice sing! When your ice-skate blade moves across the ice, it causes the ice to crack and fracture, which releases energy in the form of vibrations. These vibrations can be heard as sound-waves with lots of different frequencies. Normally in air, all the frequencies travel together, but in a solid like ice the different frequencies can get separated. This is called acoustic dispersion. The high-frequency sounds travel faster, so they reach your ears first, quickly followed by the lower-pitched sounds. This makes a noise like a laser gun from a sci-fi movie! *Pew-pew!*

You can re-create this sound in your home. Get a metal Slinky and put one end of it in a cup. Hold the cup up off the floor in one hand, and hold the other end of the Slinky in the other hand. Then, let go of the 'free' end of the Slinky – as it hits the ground, you should hear the *pew-pew* sound!

## ICE QUAKES

Ice quakes happen when water flows into frozen soil or rock and freezes suddenly because of a sudden drop in temperature. As the water freezes, it expands, and causes the rock or soil to crack!

**SOUND ON THE EARTH**

65

# SOUND in the SEA

Have you ever tried to listen to music when you're in the bath? Or maybe when you've been swimming, you've put your head under the water and heard muffled banging and shouting? If you have, then you'll understand that sounds in the sea are very different from the sounds we're used to on land. But, while humans might struggle to hear underwater, marine animals have developed some incredible techniques for communicating using sound. Let's dive in and find out more . . .

# MOTION IN THE OCEAN

We know that sound travels faster through water than it does in air, although not as fast as through a solid. When underwater objects vibrate, they cause the water molecules to vibrate too, and this creates the compressions and rarefactions (squashing and stretching) that form a sound-wave. The sound-waves can travel through the water in all directions away from the source.

Sound travels faster in warmer water, because the water particles have more energy and can vibrate faster. Cold water will create sound-waves that are slower and have much lower frequencies and longer wavelengths. And, because of their longer wavelengths, these sounds can be carried very long distances across the ocean.

## STRANGE SOUNDS UNDERWATER

Our ears work a bit differently when we are underwater, so the noises we hear sound a bit funny.

Our ears are designed to hear sounds in air by making the eardrum vibrate. Underwater, the vibrations don't need to go through the outer ear; instead they travel through the skull bones just behind the ear, then directly into the cochlea. This means we experience sound differently in water from how we do in air.

It is also harder to work out which direction the sounds are coming from. This is partly because sound travels faster in water, so the sound seems to be hitting your skull from all directions at the same time. In the air, by contrast, your ears can perceive a difference in which side or direction the sounds are coming from.

## SENSES IN THE SEA

While we might struggle to hear underwater, marine animals such as whales and dolphins have developed an amazing sensitivity to sound – which is important for helping them navigate underwater, as they can't always rely on other senses like sight or smell.

Light waves run out of energy as they travel through water, and get more and more scattered until the light is very dim, making it difficult for some animals and fish to see in the darkness of the deep ocean.

Smell can travel in a liquid and a solid, but there needs to be a high concentration of aroma particles for the smell to be detectable. In water, the concentration of aroma particles is really low, so it is harder to pinpoint smells. Some marine animals, such as sharks, do have a very powerful sense of smell and can use this to locate their prey. But dolphins have no sense of smell, so sound is even more important in helping them to navigate and hunt for food!

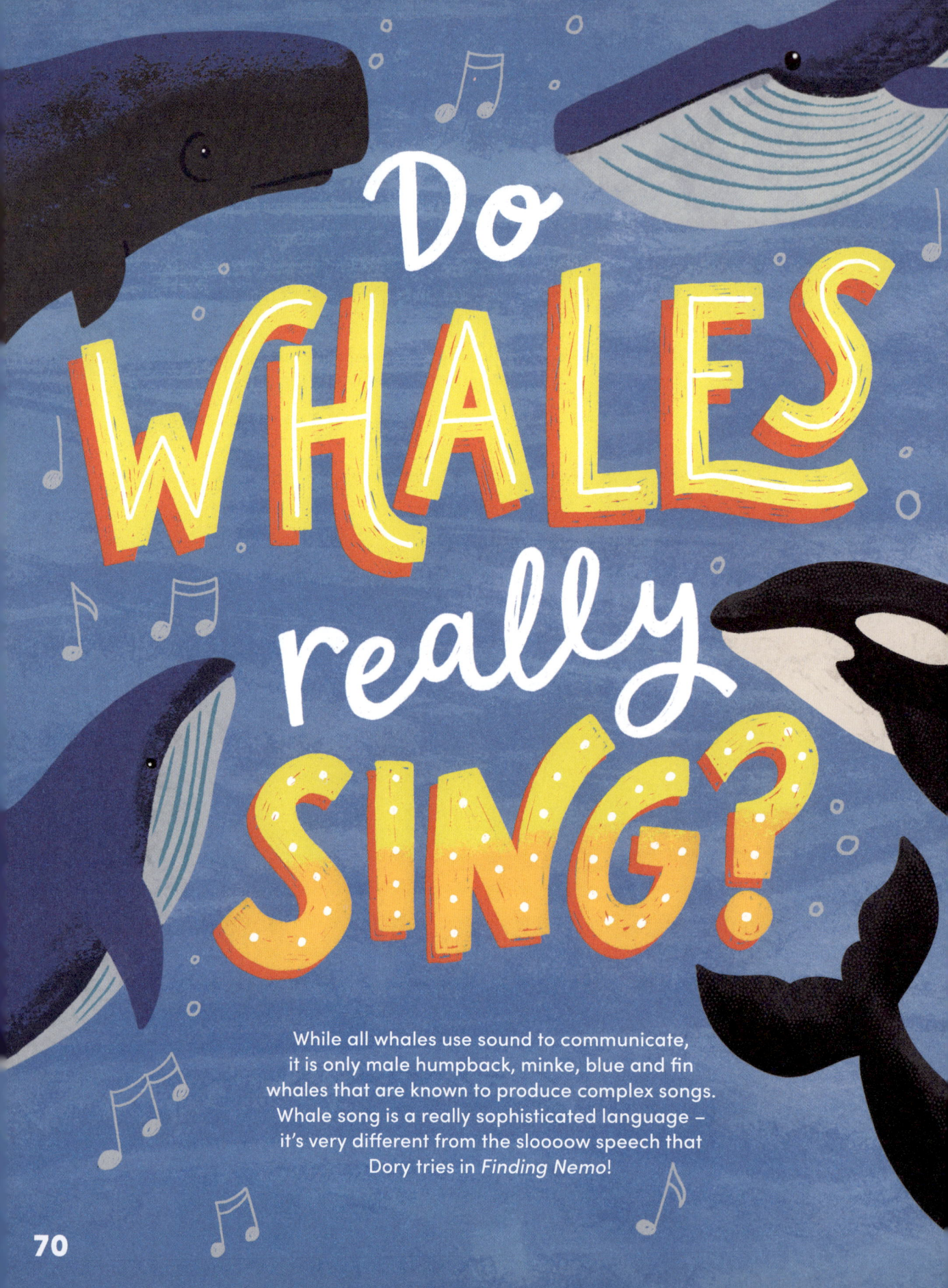

# Do WHALES really SING?

While all whales use sound to communicate, it is only male humpback, minke, blue and fin whales that are known to produce complex songs. Whale song is a really sophisticated language – it's very different from the sloooow speech that Dory tries in *Finding Nemo*!

We don't know exactly how the process works, as these huge creatures are really difficult to observe. But we do know that, a bit like human vocal cords, whales have U-shaped folds that they use to produce sound. Theirs are WAY bigger than human vocal cords though, and are thought to be much more complicated – partly because whales live and breathe underwater a lot of the time.

Scientists believe that whales have special sacs in their throats that can contain extra air, which allows them to move air between the sacs and the lungs. This means that whales can sing without running out of breath. As the sounds bounce around in the air-filled sac, they become amplified, so that the song can sound as powerful as a choir in a cathedral!

## TRACKING WHALES

Scientists can use whale song to track different types of whale, such as blue whales, which are particularly difficult to find. However, human-made noises in the ocean – from things such as boats, submarines and oil rigs – can disrupt whale song, meaning that whales can't communicate properly. And, if the noise pollution in a particular area of the ocean is too loud, whales might avoid that area altogether. This can affect their migration routes and their ability to find food or a mate. So it's important that scientists and campaign groups continue to track whales and their songs, to measure the impact of noise pollution on their survival, and to protect whale breeding and feeding grounds.

## PATTERNS IN WHALE SONG

Just like human music, each whale song has a unique structure – with different noises arranged in patterns that are repeated over and over, sometimes for hours. Whales can also change their songs by adding bits and taking bits away, and they can even teach their songs to other whales!

Whale songs can be loud enough to travel thousands of kilometres, so whales living in different habitats can sometimes pick up on other whales' songs. This process is known as cultural transmission, where learned behaviours are shared between groups that aren't related. Scientists think that male whales may sing to attract females during mating season, and to deter other males. So learning a new song might just be the way to a female whale's heart!

One blue whale with a unique singing voice has been called 'the loneliest whale in the world'. It was first recorded singing in 1989, and its songs had notes at a frequency of 52 Hz, which is at the lower end of the human hearing range and much higher-pitched than normal blue and fin whale songs.

At first, people thought this whale must be lonely, as other whales wouldn't be able to hear its song. The K-pop boy band BTS even wrote a song about the sad, solitary whale! But now we know that other whales probably could hear the lonely whale. They just might have found its song a little odd . . .

**SOUND IN THE SEA**

# WHY DO DOLPHINS MAKE A CLICKING NOISE?

Did you know dolphins are actually small whales? Dolphins and orcas (also known as killer whales) belong in the toothed whale group, while blue and humpback whales belong in the baleen whale group. Instead of teeth, baleen whales have bristly plates that collect plankton and krill for them to eat. So, all dolphins are whales, but not all whales are dolphins!

Toothed whales such as dolphins can't sing like baleen whales can. Instead, they use an amazing technique called echolocation to communicate and navigate. Echolocation allows animals to work out the location, size, shape and even the speed of an object by listening to echoes produced by sounds bouncing and reflecting off the object. This technique is so incredibly accurate that it could tell the difference between a football and a basketball from miles away!

Dolphins have sacs in their heads that can send out fast clicking noises that pass through their foreheads. These sounds are produced by air coming into the sacs from the blowhole. The air inflates the sacs, then is forced out again over something called the nasal plug, which produces the sound. Have you ever inflated a balloon, then deflated it to make a trumpeting sound? Dolphins use a similar mechanism!

The sound beam is sent out in front of the dolphin like a head torch. When the sound hits an object, it is reflected back to the dolphin's lower jaw, which has pockets filled with fat. These detect the echoes and sounds, then send the information to the middle ear and brain, where it is turned into an acoustic picture – like a map of the dolphin's surroundings made from sound.

**DID YOU KNOW?**
Each dolphin has a signature whistle, a bit like our fingerprints!

## CLEVER ORCAS

Orcas are the largest type of dolphin. They are so clever that they can copy dolphin and even human sounds! Orcas living with bottlenose dolphins were able to 'speak' the same language of clicks, which shows that they were either mimicking the dolphins or learning their language. Orcas have even been shown to be able to say 'hello' and 'bye' by copying the humans training them.

## SONAR – ECHOLOCATION FOR HUMANS!

Sonar is a way to survey and map what is underwater without having to get wet. It's a bit like a human-made form of echolocation!

The letters in the word sonar stand for SOund Navigation And Ranging. Sonar uses sound-waves and echoes to develop nautical charts and maps, find underwater hazards and search for objects on the ocean floor. Sound-waves travel further in water than light or radio waves, which is why sonar is used underwater instead of radar. Active sonar technology sends out pulses of sound into the water, which bounces off objects in the water and sends an echo back to the receiver. By working out the time between when the sound pulse was made and when the echo was heard, the sonar technology can calculate how far away the object is.

# HOW DO FISH COMMUNICATE?

Many types of fish communicate using sound – fish can grunt, click, snap and even croak! Some sounds are warnings to predators, some attract a mate, and some are made by accident as fish swim along or feed.

Fish use a few different techniques to make these noises. They can hit or rub the bony parts of their skeleton together, or use their swim bladder – basically a bag of gas that helps them to stay afloat – as a kind of drum. Some fish have a muscle called the sonic muscle attached to their swim bladder, and by squeezing this muscle against the swim bladder they can produce sound. The toadfish uses this technique to make a sound like a foghorn!

Sharks can also use the accidental sounds that fish make to find food. A school of fish may make a low-frequency sound just by swimming along together. Sharks can detect these low-frequency sounds and follow them to find dinner!

## SNAPPING SHRIMPS

Snapping shrimp (also known as pistol shrimp) are famous for producing one of the loudest sounds in the ocean. These small but mighty creatures have one claw much bigger than the other, and use the bigger claw to make a loud popping noise to communicate, warn off predators and even stun prey. When the claw snaps open and shut, it creates a big bubble in the water. The bubble breaks with a loud *POP!* It's a bit like the shrimp shooting a pistol underwater, and can shock prey enough to be able to give the shrimp time to grab it and eat it!

# EXPLORING THE SEA-FLOOR

The sea-floor is a very mysterious place. In fact, we know more about the surface of Mars than we do about our own planet's underwater realm!

Geologists, the scientists who study rocks and the Earth, are using sound-waves to map the sea-floor, and to analyse rocks and sediment – pieces of land that have been broken down into smaller bits, such as sand, mud or pebbles. The sea-floor is made up of layer upon layer of sediment that has built up over time, and studying these layers can give geologists a snapshot of what the Earth used to be like.

Geologists can use sound to explore the sea-floor in a few different ways.

- **Seismic reflection** sends low-frequency sound pulses into the sea-floor, and measures how much sound energy is reflected back into a receiver.

- **Seismic refraction** measures how sound pulses are bent in different directions as they pass through different layers of sediment, which tells geologists how dense the layers are.

- **Echosounding** uses an instrument to send low-frequency sound-waves to the bottom of the ocean that are then reflected back as echoes. Scientists can work out how deep the ocean is by timing how long it takes for the echo to be heard by the receiver on board a ship at the surface.

SOUND IN THE SEA

# SOUNDS of the DEEP

Thanks to underwater microphones and other 'listening equipment' in the ocean, we have been eavesdropping on the deep sea for many years. In 1997, a mysterious noise called the Bloop was detected. It lasted about one minute and started as a low rumbling noise, ending with a higher-pitched bloop sound!

## THE BLOOP

Over time, scientists worked out that the approximate location for the Bloop was the Antarctic, and that the sound might have been made by huge icebergs splitting in two and falling into the freezing sea.

Over the years, icebergs have made some very weird noises indeed – from a cooing noise possibly caused by an iceberg scratching along the sea-floor to a screeching noise that sounded like train wheels on a track!

## IS ANYBODY DOWN THERE?

Even more mysterious sounds have emerged from the deepest, darkest place in the ocean, the Mariana Trench. This deep, crescent-shaped dent, located in the Pacific Ocean, is the deepest ocean trench on Earth. The lowest point is known as Challenger Deep and is deep enough to fit an upside-down Mount Everest, with room to spare!

In 2016, researchers heard groaning, moaning, grumbling and screeching coming from Challenger Deep. The sounds were heard over 23 days by a specialized microphone that was lowered into the trench. Most of the noises were attributed to boats, earthquakes and different types of whale. But some are still unaccounted for! There is so much we don't know yet about the Mariana Trench and what could be down there . . .

## THE SOUND OF WATER

The sounds of water can have various effects on the human body. Some people listen to waves crashing to calm them into a deep sleep, while others find that water trickling makes them feel like they need a wee! But why does this happen?

## WHEN YOU GOTTA GO!

Scientists haven't worked out exactly why some of us need a wee after hearing or seeing running water, but it is likely to be because of a conditioned response. This is when humans or animals become trained to react to something in a particular way, or to automatically link two things together. For example, a dog might get excited when they see their owner pick up their lead, because it means they're probably going for a walk. As humans, we become used to hearing the sound of running water when we are in the bathroom, so this sound automatically reminds us of needing the loo!

## SOOTHING WAVES

The sound of water can also help to soothe and calm us. From crashing waves to babbling brooks to the pitter-patter of rain to the ebb and flow of the tides, flowing water can send us to sleep. It is believed that these steady, slow, repetitive and non-threatening sounds can trigger a response in our brain that makes us feel safe and relaxed. Watery noises can also block out unwanted background noise, such as traffic or police sirens.

# SOUND in the SKY

We've seen how sounds move through the Earth and the ocean. Now, let's take flight and listen for sounds up in the sky! From planes that break the sound barrier to birds that use sound to hunt for prey, there are plenty of sounds for us to discover in the clouds.

# BEATING AND BUZZING

Insects make noises in lots of different ways, from beating their wings to buzzing around! Sometimes they make noise accidentally, other times it is a warning to keep well away, and sometimes their songs are a mating call. Moths, such as tiger moths and hawk moths, make rapid ultrasonic clicks in order to put off predators like bats. They make these clicks by rubbing their body parts together in a process called stridulation.

Flies and bees make buzzing noises using their wings and muscles. Flies sound as though they are humming because they flap their wings 200 times per second, which makes them sound like mini helicopters! And did you know that buzzing can help bees to pollinate plants? The vibrations loosen the pollen, which is transferred on to a bee, and the bee then takes the pollen to another flower. But sometimes the buzzing can also be a sign to other creatures to stay away.

BEE

# OUCH!

Talking of buzzing . . . how itchy do you feel even thinking about a buzzing mosquito? A mosquito's wings can beat up to 600 times per second! This movement causes vibrations in the air that you hear as a buzzy, whiney sound that means only one thing: you're on the menu tonight!

But why do mosquitoes buzz in our ears? We think it is because the pests are attracted to carbon dioxide and heat – both of which come from us as we exhale, or breathe out! So, perhaps the bugs aren't specifically attracted to our ears, but just our heads in general. And it is only female mosquitos that bite humans! So, that high-pitched whine is coming from the female of the species.

Mozzies can change the pitch of their buzz depending on how fast they flap their wings. The faster the flap, the higher-pitched the sound – and they often do this when they are pursuing a mate!

MOSQUITO

FLY

TIGER MOTH

HAWK MOTH

**DID YOU KNOW?**
Flies can't hear any kind of sound – not even their own buzzing!

SOUND IN THE SKY

# HUNTING FOR PREY

Owls have much better hearing than other birds, which means they are very effective at listening out for their favourite dinner! Since owls are nocturnal, they can't rely on sight to find prey – instead, they use their excellent hearing.

Owls' ears are completely within their heads (they don't have flappy outer ears like we do), and their feathers ruffle up around their face to channel sound into them. Their faces are also disc-shaped to focus sound, a bit like tiny satellite dishes! One ear is bigger than the other, and the left one is set lower on their heads than the other. Since their ears aren't in a straight line, sound reaches one ear first, then the other – and this allows owls to pinpoint the location of sounds better than if their ears were aligned.

Owls have outer, middle and inner ears, and eardrums that are bigger than that of any other bird. They have just one bone in the inner ear (instead of three like humans), but the way they hear is similar to how humans hear. The sound-waves in the air are converted by the eardrum and bone into vibrations, which make thousands of tiny hairs in the inner ear move. Different hairs move for different-frequency sounds, and this helps the owl's brain to create a picture of the sounds it can hear.

Owls are able to use their amazing hearing to work out where exactly prey is, even when they can't see it. And, because owls tend to stay in the same habitat for their whole lives, they get to know their surroundings really well – so this combined with their super hearing makes them deadly accurate hunters!

SOUND IN THE SKY

# BATS, OILBIRDS and ECHOES

Bats and cave-dwelling South American oilbirds use echolocation just like toothed whales do, to avoid predators and communicate with each other. Bats use high-pitched sounds that are inaudible to the human ear to help them find food, such as insects.

Oilbirds use low-pitched sounds that we can hear to work out how big their caves are. When it is really dark, an oilbird sends out a clever pattern of low-frequency clicks that it creates by contracting (or squashing) the muscles inside their bronchial tubes (a set of tubes connected to their lungs), which forces the air out. The clicks bounce off the cave walls back to the bird's ears, and it can work out how big its cave is.

Low-frequency noises have long wavelengths, which means the sounds an oilbird makes can only detect larger objects – the smallest possible object it can detect is about the size of a grape. Luckily, oilbirds enjoy eating grapes, so that's OK! The larger objects deflect the sound-waves more, which helps the birds to work out the size, shape and location of any obstacle in their way.

Oilbirds can't echolocate as well as bats can, partly because of the low-frequency clicks. The lower the frequency of a sound, the less crisp and clear it is. Scientists believe oilbirds can avoid objects bigger than 10 centimetres in size, but the ability of their echolocation to work accurately gets a bit murky after about 20 centimetres. But it is still good enough to stop them from crashing into cave walls!

## AS SHARP-EARED AS A BAT

Bats make their high-pitched sounds using their larynxes. These sounds come out of their mouths as extremely loud and high-pitched screams. Luckily, we can't hear the sounds, because they can go up to 140 dB – which would be like listening to a jet engine from 30 metres away! A bat's echolocation is so good that it can build up a picture of an insect 5 metres away, and it can also work out the size of the insect and whether or not it has a hard body. Bats can even avoid wires as thin as human hair!

## DID YOU KNOW?

Bats could deafen themselves if they heard their own noises! To prevent this from happening, bats can 'switch off' their middle ear – and turn it back on again to receive the echoes.

**SOUND IN THE SKY**

# WHY DOES THUNDER RUMBLE?

**DID YOU KNOW?**
Since light travels faster than sound, you will see lightning before you hear thunder!

You might think that thunder and lightning are two separate things, but thunder is actually the sound that lightning makes!

Only thunder-clouds can make thunder and lightning. Thunder-clouds are very tall, although we can't see how tall they are from Earth. They are a type of cloud called cumulonimbus, which means they are huge and puffy, with flat bottoms.

Clouds are made from water vapour and air, and these very tall ones reach high up in the sky. This means that the top of the cloud is very cold, and the water vapour starts to freeze into ice crystals inside the clouds. Ice is lighter and less dense than water, so the cloud begins to separate into ice towards the top and water towards the bottom.

The ice and water move past each other and rub, creating static electricity – which is the same force that causes a balloon to stick to your hair when you've rubbed it on your head! Static electricity makes the ice crystals become positively charged and the water negatively charged. The part of the water particle that is negatively charged is called an electron. Since negative charges repel one another, the electrons all flow away from each other, travelling downwards towards the Earth.

This motion of electrons is what we call electricity. As soon as the negatively charged electrons reach the surface of the Earth, a lightning flash is created!

The lightning heats the air around it, and when you heat air it expands. The air around the lightning expands so fast that a shock wave is created – a bit like in a sonic boom (see page 90) – and the shock wave is the thunder!

If you hear thunder as a crack, then the lightning is very close by. If you hear the rumble of thunder, the lightning is further away from you. If you see the lightning and hear the thunder almost together, the storm is very close by.

## SOUND IN THE SKY

**WARNING!**

Lightning is very dangerous, so if you are outside and you hear thunder, especially if it's a loud crack, go inside!

### ELECTRIC AURORA

The northern and southern lights, or *aurora borealis/aurora australis*, are a beautiful phenomenon that occurs in the uppermost parts of the northern and southern hemispheres. They are caused by energetic particles from the Sun interacting with the particles in our atmosphere, creating curtains of stunning, glowing lights in the sky. When conditions are very still and very clear, a sizzling, crackling, popping sound can be heard in chorus to the aurora! Scientists believe that the noises are from the electrical charges within the aurora creating small sparks.

# SONIC BOOM!

> **DID YOU KNOW?**
> The supersonic plane Concorde only took around three hours to travel from London, in the United Kingdom, to New York, in the United States – an average flight from London to New York is 8 hours!

A sonic boom is a noise a bit like the rumble of thunder that is caused by something moving faster than the speed of sound. The speed of sound at average air temperature (18 degrees Celsius) – is about 340 metres per second, and lots of modern aircraft can travel faster than this!

An aeroplane moving through the atmosphere is similar to a boat sailing through water. At the nose of the aeroplane, the air is compressed, creating air-pressure waves like the waves of water created at a ship's bow. If the plane is flying slower than the speed of sound, the sound-waves can ripple outwards from the plane. This is why we can hear a roaring noise in the sky when a plane passes us. We can't see the sound-waves, but you can sometimes see the effect they have on the clouds in the sky overhead.

If the plane speeds up and travels faster than the speed of sound, the sound-waves get in the way of the plane! The sound-waves can't move away fast enough and get all bunched up together until a shock wave is formed. The shock wave creates a V-shape behind the plane, like you might see in water waves behind a boat. This shock wave creates the sonic-boom sound you hear as the aeroplane passes. Aeroplanes travelling faster than the speed of sound are said to be travelling at supersonic speeds.

The sound barrier, or sonic barrier, is not an actual barrier in the sky, but the sudden increase in drag on the aircraft as it approaches the speed of sound. When aircraft were first created, they couldn't come close to the speed of sound, as the sound barrier would drag on the plane and make it impossible to travel any faster. But modern aircraft can travel at much higher speeds!

## THE FIRST SUPERSONIC FLIGHT

The first ever plane to travel faster than the speed of sound was nicknamed *Glamorous Glennis*. It was piloted by Captain Chuck Yeager, and on 14 October 1947 travelled at Mach 1.06. (Mach 1 is the speed of sound at sea level on a normal day, which is 343 metres per second. Mach 2 would be twice the speed of sound.)

To break the sound barrier, the plane had to be really aerodynamic, or specially designed so that it moved easily through the air. It had thin, strong wings and looked a bit like a streamlined bullet, but with wings and a very pointy nose!

Captain Yeager was the most experienced test pilot in the United States Air Force at the time. No other planes had flown faster than the speed of sound before, and there was a danger that the sound barrier could be so strong that the aircraft could be destroyed mid-flight. But Yeager was determined to try to break the barrier, and his incredible achievement proved that humans could travel faster than the speed of sound without it being harmful or dangerous to our health. This was important for the future of space flight and astronauts travelling off the surface of the Earth.

SOUND IN THE SKY

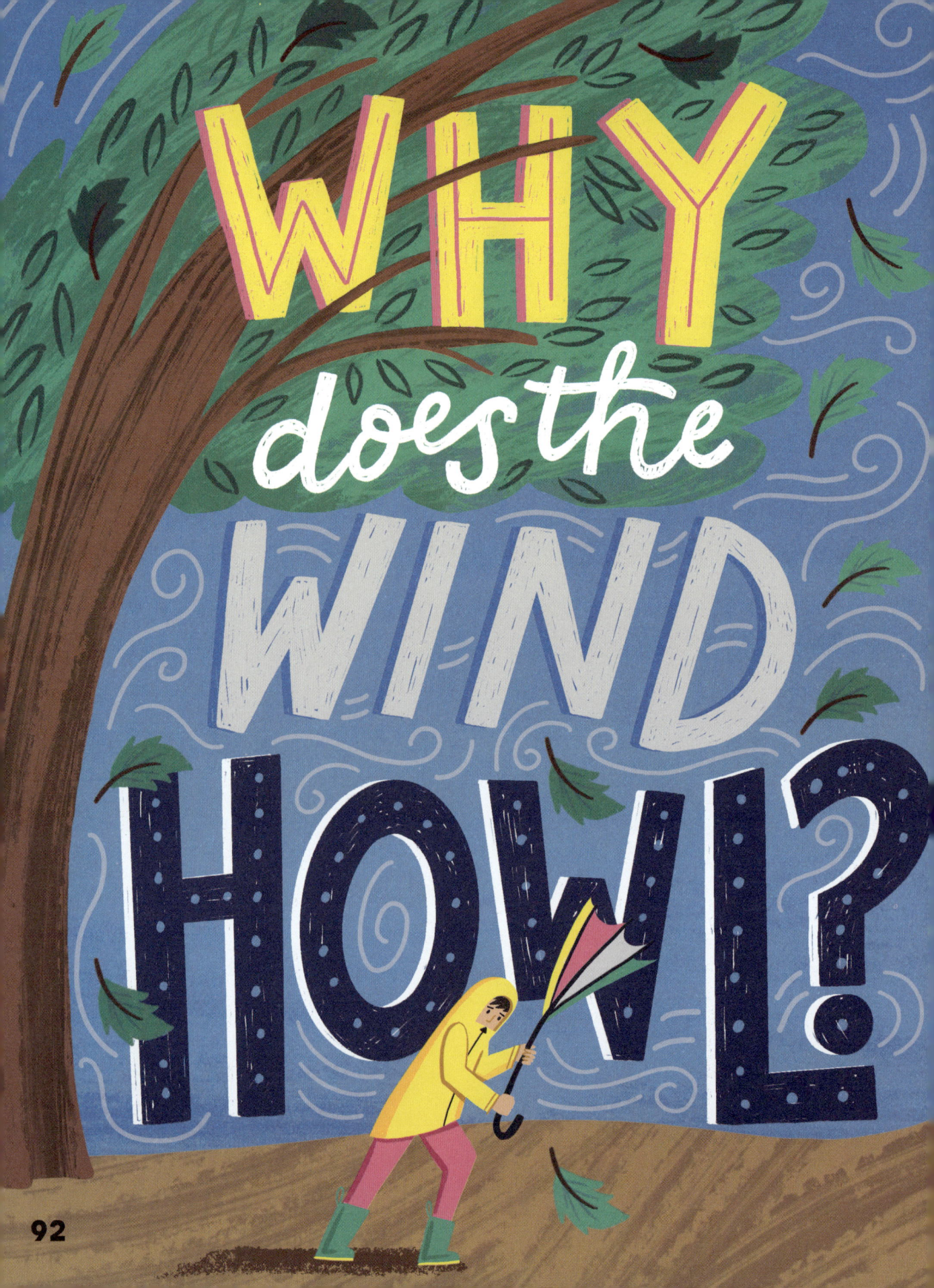

On a particularly blustery day, you might hear an eerie howling sound. It's not a ghost – though it can be pretty spooky! Rather, it's a sound effect of the wind. But what is the wind, and why does it howl?

Air pressure is a way of measuring the weight of air above us in the atmosphere – the blanket of gases that surround our planet, keeping us warm and giving us oxygen to breathe. The atmosphere is where Earth's weather happens.

The warmer the air in the atmosphere is, the more energy the particles have. This means they vibrate more, and move apart from each other. There are therefore fewer air particles in any given space, meaning that the warm air is lighter and less dense – and, since the air is lighter, there is less pressure pushing down on to the surface below.

Colder air has less energy, so the particles move around less and are closer together, making the air heavier – so it presses downwards with greater pressure.

← AIR PARTICLES

## WHAT CREATES WIND?

The Earth is heated unevenly by the Sun. The water and land at the equator – the imaginary line that runs round the centre of the globe, at an equal distance from the North Pole and the South Pole – is warmer than the water and land in other parts of the planet. The warmer air is low pressure, and the cooler air is high pressure.

The warmer, low-pressure air rises in the atmosphere and travels towards the poles. As the warm air moves upwards, it is replaced by cooler, higher-pressure air. This movement of air – caused by the uneven heating of the Earth by the Sun – creates wind. Wind blows mostly from high-pressure to low-pressure areas.

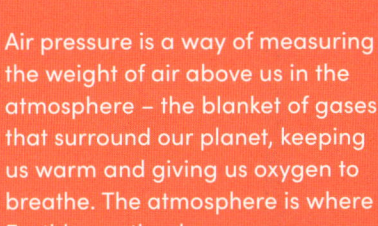

## OOOOOO!

When wind blows through a forest, it flows around objects in its path, such as trees. The wind is split, moves around the object, then comes back together on the other side of the object. The wind doesn't split evenly, though, so the wind on one side of the tree will be stronger than on the other side. When the wind streams come back together, the stronger wind mixes with the weaker wind. This causes vibrations in the air, which produce the howling noise that we find spooky!

The vibrations created by wind are absorbed by things like leaves on trees. This is why, in the northern hemisphere, we hear spooky howling noises at Hallowe'en in autumn, when there are fewer leaves on the trees than in the middle of summer.

**SOUND IN THE SKY**

# SOUND in SPACE

We've been on quite a journey through this book, from the bottom of the Mariana Trench up into the Earth's atmosphere. We've learned about strange sounds in the sea, clever ways animals use sound to navigate, and the weird and wonderful weather noises made by lightning. All that's left is for us to jet off into outer space!

# CAN SOUND TRAVEL IN SPACE?

We know that sound-waves need particles to transfer energy through vibrations. But, apart from massive objects such as planets, moons and stars, there isn't much 'stuff' in space. Outer space is so huge and so spread out that there is almost nothing there.

We call space a vacuum because there are no air molecules – it's almost like someone has literally taken a vacuum cleaner and sucked them out! And, since there are no particles in outer space, if a sound *is* created, there is no matter to transfer the sound energy through vibrations, so it cannot be heard.

Remember the saying 'in space, no one can hear you scream'? Well, this would only be true if you were talking about *outer* space. In outer space, you would still be able to scream and make a noise . . . but the sounds can't be transferred, so any beings capable of hearing you wouldn't be able to pick the scream up!

But that doesn't mean space as a whole is quiet. Just like the bottom of the ocean, if you eavesdrop on space, you'll find there are noises everywhere!

## SOUNDS ON THE INTERNATIONAL SPACE STATION

On the International Space Station (ISS), air is pumped in to allow the astronauts living on board to breathe. This means there are particles to vibrate, and sounds can be heard by the astronauts.

The ISS is actually an incredibly noisy place! There is a constant whirr of fans, pumps and other machines. Since there is noise all the time, the astronauts have to be carefully monitored for any changes or damage to their hearing. Astronauts used to wear earplugs or headphones to protect themselves, but as technology has improved the machines have become less noisy, so astronauts don't always need to wear hearing protection. But they do need to sleep in sound-proof quarters to let their ears have a break!

SOUND IN SPACE

The International Space Station is a large spacecraft where astronauts live and work. This means it travels around the Earth in a regular path. Earth's gravity is what keeps the ISS around it.

# CAN WE DETECT SOUND IN OUTER SPACE?

The Big Bang was the moment at which our entire universe was created, around 13.8 billion years ago. Scientists think the universe started from a single, extremely dense point, then expanded outwards – and it is still expanding today.

Sound-waves can't travel in outer space, but radio waves can, because they don't need a medium to travel through. Radio waves can be captured by powerful radio telescopes and turned into sound – which means that scientists can listen to stars, galaxies, and even the sounds that were created in the Big Bang!

A radio telescope collects radio waves in a huge dish, which acts as an antenna, and focuses the waves on to a receiver and amplifier to boost the radio signals. Then, a recorder collects the information about the radio signal.

Astronomers can use radio signals to detect some of the oldest sounds in space. Almost immediately after the Big Bang, some of the first bits of matter to form were hydrogen particles. These hydrogen particles in the early universe had a neutral charge – meaning they were not positive or negative. Neutral hydrogen atoms emit radio waves at a certain frequency, which can be converted into sound using powerful radio telescopes. Incredibly, this means scientists can detect signals from neutral hydrogen in faraway galaxies that are billions of years old.

## WHAT DO PIGEONS HAVE TO DO WITH THE BIG BANG?

In 1964, astronomers Robert W. Wilson and Arno A. Penzias were working with a radio telescope at a laboratory in New Jersey, in the United States, when they noticed a strange hissing noise. Wilson and Penzias searched for the source of the noise, and discovered two pigeons living inside the big, horn-shaped antenna of the telescope. At first, they figured the pigeons must be the source of the noise, but after they'd caught the pigeons and cleaned the equipment the noise was still there. The astronomers realized that the sound wasn't coming from anywhere nearby, but was in fact something called Cosmic Microwave Background Radiation (or CMBR).

CBMR is a bit like an echo from the massive explosion of energy that happened during the Big Bang. It's what was left over from the first light that ever travelled through the universe. Over billions of years, this energy has cooled and now exists as microwaves, which are at the higher-frequency end of radio waves on the electromagnetic spectrum. Scientists can convert these wavelengths into sound – meaning it's possible for them to listen in on the birth of the universe!

The biggest radio telescope is the Five-hundred-meter Aperture Spherical Telescope, or FAST, located in Guizhou province, in China. It's wider than the Eiffel Tower!

RADIO TELESCOPE

SOUND IN SPACE

# THE SOUND OF THE SUN

If we could hear the Sun, it would be like being at a rock concert! The Sun emits charged particles and gas, and these are constantly rising, falling, cooling, heating and moving. If there wasn't a vacuum in between the Sun and Earth, we would hear these effects as sound – and it would probably sound something like a roaring waterfall!

## SOHO

While we can't actually hear the Sun from Earth, there is a spacecraft that can translate its movements into sound. The Solar and Heliospheric Observatory (SOHO) is stationed around 1.5 million kilometres from Earth, where it slowly orbits the Sun, taking photographs and recording data. SOHO also captures the vibrations created by the eruptions, waves, and dynamic movement of the Sun, and processes the data to make it audible to humans. The data from SOHO has even been used to create an immersive art installation called Solarium, where viewers are surrounded by the imagery and sounds of our Sun!

# SOUND IN SPACE

You should never look directly at the Sun as it can damage your eyes! Scientists need to use special equipment to allow them to observe the Sun safely.

Helioseismology is similar to seismology, the study of earthquakes, but for the Sun! Helios means 'sun' in Ancient Greek. We can use helioseismology to learn more about the Sun in the same way that scientists use earthquakes to learn more about the Earth. And scientists use similar methods to learn about other stars – this is called asteroseismology!

THE SOLAR AND HELIOSPHERIC OBSERVATORY

101

# SINGING STARS!

You might have sung 'Twinkle, Twinkle, Little Star' when you were little, but did you know that stars can actually sing?

← CONVECTION CURRENT

Just like our Sun, which is a type of star, all stars naturally create noise, due to the heating and moving of gases. Different stars are able to make different sounds depending on how big they are. Inside stars, the gases heat up and cool down in something called a convection current. The convection current creates waves inside the star, which cause the star to pulse. This gentle pulsing can be turned into audio frequencies via radio telescopes, so astronomers can hear the stars singing!

Most stars pulse gently, and their brightness can change a bit. Our Sun's brightness may change by up to 1 per cent over an eleven-year period. However, some stars change brightness a lot – enough that we can see the changes from Earth. We call these types of stars variable stars.

## PULSARS

Certain types of neutron star spin round really fast and emit pulses of radiation along the star's magnetic poles. (Radiation is energy – such as light, sound, heat or X-rays – that moves from one place to another.) As the star spins, the beams of radiation coming from its poles rotate too. From Earth, we can detect the beams as radio waves flickering on and off, like a lighthouse beam.

When a beam isn't pointing towards Earth, we can't detect it, but as the star spins the beam will point towards Earth . . . then away again. This forms a pulsing pattern, which is why these neutron stars are also called **pulsars!** The range of pulses can vary from milliseconds to seconds, but each one is so regular you could set your watch to it.

## NEUTRON STARS

Neutron stars are dying stars, which form when massive stars that are much bigger than our Sun run out of fuel. The central core of the star collapses in on itself, and crushes all the particles into a dense ball of neutral particles called neutrons. This makes the core extremely dense and extremely heavy. A sugar-cube amount of neutron-star core would weigh about the same as a large mountain!

## NOISY STARS

A long, long time ago, a variable star called Mira was recorded changing brightness. An astronomer called David Fabricius documented this in 1596, but we think that ancient Babylonian, Chinese and Greek scientists might have noticed it way before then! And amazingly, Mira still pulses today.

There are other 'noisy' stars too, such as Alpha Centauri A, which pulses so fast that its surface rises and falls with a frequency of about 35 centimetres each second. We can measure these pulses, turn the signal into sound, and take a listen to these amazing objects in the universe.

## DID YOU KNOW?

When the first pulsars were detected by Northern Irish astrophysicist Jocelyn Bell Burnell, the heartbeat-like pulse of the radio waves was so mysterious that scientists nicknamed it LGM-1, which stands for 'little green men' – a.k.a. aliens!

SOUND IN SPACE

# LISTENING OUT FOR ALIENS

*Perhaps aliens might find us by listening to our radio transmissions? What songs should we send them to tell them we're here? I'd send something like 'What a Wonderful World' by Louis Armstrong. What would you send?*

Do you believe in aliens? If you could hear them, what do you think they might sound like? And if they did visit and start to communicate, how might we communicate back? What if aliens were so intelligent that they could read what you were thinking . . . that would be a bit concerning!

If it were possible to communicate with aliens, then radio waves could be the best way to do it, as we know it is possible to detect radio waves from galaxies billions of years away. The idea of using radio waves to search for aliens has actually been around for over a hundred years.

- In the early 1900s, Serbian-American inventor Nikola Tesla – who made huge developments in radio technology – claimed that he had received radio transmissions from Mars.

- In 1924, the United States government declared a National Radio Silence Day, when all radio transmissions were to be turned off for five minutes every hour so that astronomers could listen out for aliens. Nothing was heard!

- In 1959, an American project called the Search for Extra-terrestrial Intelligence, or SETI, was launched. The SETI project uses radio telescopes around the world to sweep the skies, looking for radio-wave signals in space that could have been created by alien lifeforms.

## GOLDEN RECORDS

Two golden phonograph records (also known as gramophone records – remember them from page 37?) were sent on NASA's *Voyager 1* and *Voyager 2* space-probe missions in 1977 (one on each spacecraft). The records were a copy of each other, and contained 116 images, plus music and sounds that were thought to represent human life at the time. The idea was that *Voyager 1* and *Voyager 2* might pass into another solar system, where aliens could find the records, see the images and hear the sounds – and know everything they needed to about us!

The records had pictures engraved into showing DNA, a human heart and lungs, the structure of the Earth, trees, crocodiles and an astronaut in space. And there were even pictures that would tell anyone who found the records exactly how to play them – some extra-terrestrial instructions!

The records also contained ninety minutes of music from different historical times and cultures, including classical music by Bach and Mozart, and traditional music from Peru, India, Zaire and Japan.

SOUND IN SPACE

# STRANGE SOUNDS ON SATURN

Next on our tour of sounds in the solar system is my favourite planet . . . Saturn! Saturn is a wild and fascinating world, with rings and moons that really capture the imagination, and it's full of unusual sounds that scientists are still discovering more about. But first, let's learn a bit more about the planet itself . . .

## THE PLANET SATURN

Saturn is the second-largest planet in our solar system, and is a gas giant, which means it is mainly made up of helium and hydrogen swirling round a solid core. Saturn is about nine times the width of the Earth! Most of the knowledge we have about Saturn comes from the *Cassini* spacecraft and its passenger, the *Huygens* probe, which was launched in 1997.

## THUNDERSTORMS ON SATURN

Just like Earth, Saturn has storms, lightning and thunder. Scientists have even seen and heard a thunderstorm on Saturn that has lasted for more than eight months!

The lightning generated on Saturn can be 10,000 times stronger than lightning here on Earth. The reason the storms are so powerful is because the layers of gas get completely disrupted, and the clouds are driven upwards like a gaseous volcano, spewing water ice into Saturn's atmosphere. This process is very similar to how Earth's thunderstorms are created – but Saturn is much bigger, and has a lot more atmosphere, so the thunder-clouds are twenty times taller and much wider, with winds that can reach up to 500 kilometres per hour! The thunder itself sounds very crackly and popping, not the deep rumble that we have on Earth.

### MANY MOONS

Saturn has an incredible 146 moons! And they are amazingly varied, with some bigger than the planet Mercury and others just 2.5 kilometres across.

SOUND IN SPACE

107

# THE SOUND OF SATURN'S RINGS

Saturn's rings are millions of kilometres wide, and made from ice, dust, rocks and small grains of material. But they are also extremely thin compared to how wide they are – only hundreds of kilometres deep – so, if you see the rings side on, they appear as a thin line across Saturn's equator.

By studying the magnetic field and gravity around Saturn's rings, scientists can tell that there are seismic waves coming from inside the planet out into the rings. This creates tiny tremors in the rings, which cause the ring particles to vibrate and make waves. When converted to audio, the vibrating rings sound like a bell chiming! The study of these tremors is called ring seismology!

The Radio and Plasma Wave Science (RPWS) was able to receive and detect radio emissions, lightning and dust, among other things, coming from Saturn, then convert that information into sound that was possible to hear.

There are more than twenty different types of wave in Saturn's rings, and they were first detected by the Cassini spacecraft. Cassini even flew in between Saturn and its rings, where there was nothing but empty silence!

Some planets, including Earth and Saturn, have a magnetic field. If you've ever played with a magnet, you will have seen a magnetic field on a smaller scale – this is the area around the magnet in which other magnets or magnetic material are attracted to it. Earth has a magnetic field because it has a layer of hot liquid iron and nickel close to its centre, known as the outer core. The movement of the outer core is what causes Earth's magnetic field, which extends outwards into space. We don't know as much about Saturn's magnetic field as we do about Earth's, but scientists think this is also created by liquid material flowing around in the centre of the planet.

# Saturn's Chatty Moon

During one of *Cassini*'s final orbits round Saturn, scientists detected plasma waves moving between the planet and the moon Enceladus. Plasma is a 'soup' of charged particles, which can become energized and move in a wave formation. Plasma waves can be converted into sound-waves that we can hear. They sound quite eerie, with whooping and scratching as the planet and the moon interact. It's almost as though Saturn and Enceladus are chatting to each other!

## SOUND-WAVES ON TITAN

The sounds of Titan, another of Saturn's moons, were collected in 2005 when *Huygens* landed on its surface. And, on this particular landing, the probe collected actual sound-waves with microphones – not radio waves that were converted to audio! The audio data allowed scientists to hear what it might sound like to travel through the cloudy haze and even bump down on to the moon's surface. The data was sent back to *Cassini*, which eventually used its radio transmitter to send the information back to Earth.

## MUSIC FROM SATURN'S AURORA

Saturn has a spectacular aurora, which forms in exactly the same way as the aurora on Earth – but on a much bigger scale! The solar wind from the Sun is made up of charged particles that interact with Saturn's magnetic field. These particles give off radio waves as they travel in spirals down the magnetic field towards the planet.

With the instruments on *Cassini*, scientists were able to 'listen' to the magnetic field, the radio waves and the plasma waves at Saturn's aurora. The complicated rising and falling tones sounded similar to the ghostly sounds of the aurora on Earth!

## LISTENING TO GANYMEDE

It's not just Saturn's moons that we have recorded. Jupiter's moons also emit waves that can be turned into sounds!

The spacecraft orbiting Jupiter is called *Juno* and it has a Waves instrument, which measures radio waves and plasma waves detected from Jupiter and its moons. The Waves instrument was able to 'listen' to Ganymede, one of Jupiter's moons, which is the largest moon in the solar system. Ganymede emits waves that sound like an eerie crackling, whistling noise when put into the audible range. For any grown-ups reading this, Ganymede sounds like dial-up internet! (If you were born later than about the year 2000, you won't know what dial-up sounds like, but it was basically a very whistly, crackling noise that computers used to make when connecting to the internet.)

Ganymede has a magnetic field of its own, which scientists think could be because the moon has a liquid-iron core, but it's still a bit of a mystery. It was discovered in 1996 by NASA's *Galileo* space probe. And we're hoping that the European Space Agency's Jupiter *Icy Moons Explorer* (a.k.a. Juice), which launched in 2023 and is expected to orbit at Ganymede by 2034, will shed more light on this strange moon!

## DID YOU KNOW?

The *Juno* spacecraft has three miniature 'astronauts' on board – three LEGO™ figurines made from aluminium instead of plastic! The reason they were made out of aluminium is because it's stronger and will last much longer than plastic, and won't melt or freeze under extreme temperatures.

**SOUND IN SPACE**

# MORE STRANGE SOUNDS IN SPACE . . .

We've listened in on some noisy stars, planets, spacecraft and even the Big Bang, but what other strange sounds might be out there?

## THE SOUND OF A BLACK HOLE

Scientists have recently been able to capture the noises coming from a black hole in a galaxy millions of light years away!

A black hole is the result of a very huge star dying. When a huge star runs out of fuel, it expands and cools, before suddenly exploding in something called a supernova. After the supernova, the star collapses in on itself, and creates a black hole, which not even light can escape from. If the star was really big, the gravity force of the black hole will be huge, too. Black holes are invisible, but we can measure the radiation that is created as the black hole sucks in matter. This radiation forms jets that fire out of the black hole like laser beams!

Millions of light years from our Milky Way, in the Perseus cluster of galaxies, these jets of radiation smack into gas around the galaxy cluster. This collision causes ripples, like when you throw a stone into a lake. These ripples are known as pressure waves, and they are basically sound-waves that no one can hear. The compressions and rarefactions (squashing and stretching) are present, but there are no particles to transport the sound. However, these pressure waves can be converted to sound using technology back on Earth.

Scientists believe that this black hole in the Perseus cluster is humming at the lowest and deepest note in the universe! If we could hear it, this note would sound like a musical note 57 octaves below middle C – or more than a million billion times deeper than what humans can hear!

## SOUND IN SPACE

> A light year is the distance that light travels in one year – one light year equals about 9.46 trillion kilometres. Our Sun is 149 million kilometres away from Earth – but that is only 8 light minutes away, a tiny fraction of a light year!

## THE SINGING COMET

Instruments on the *Rosetta* spacecraft were able to pick up sounds coming from Comet 67P. A **comet** is a bit like a huge, dirty snowball in the outer solar system. Comets are made up of ice, rock and dust, with a long tail of gas that looks like a streak across the night sky. There are 'short-period' comets that take less than 200 years to orbit the Sun and 'long-period' comets that take over 200 years – and in some cases, up to 1 million years!

Comet 67P is giving off waves at about 50 mHz, which is below the range of human hearing. But, by increasing the frequency, scientists were able to hear these sounds – and they discovered that the comet seems to be singing its heart out! The song sounds like a mix between dolphin clicks, taps and whirrs.

113

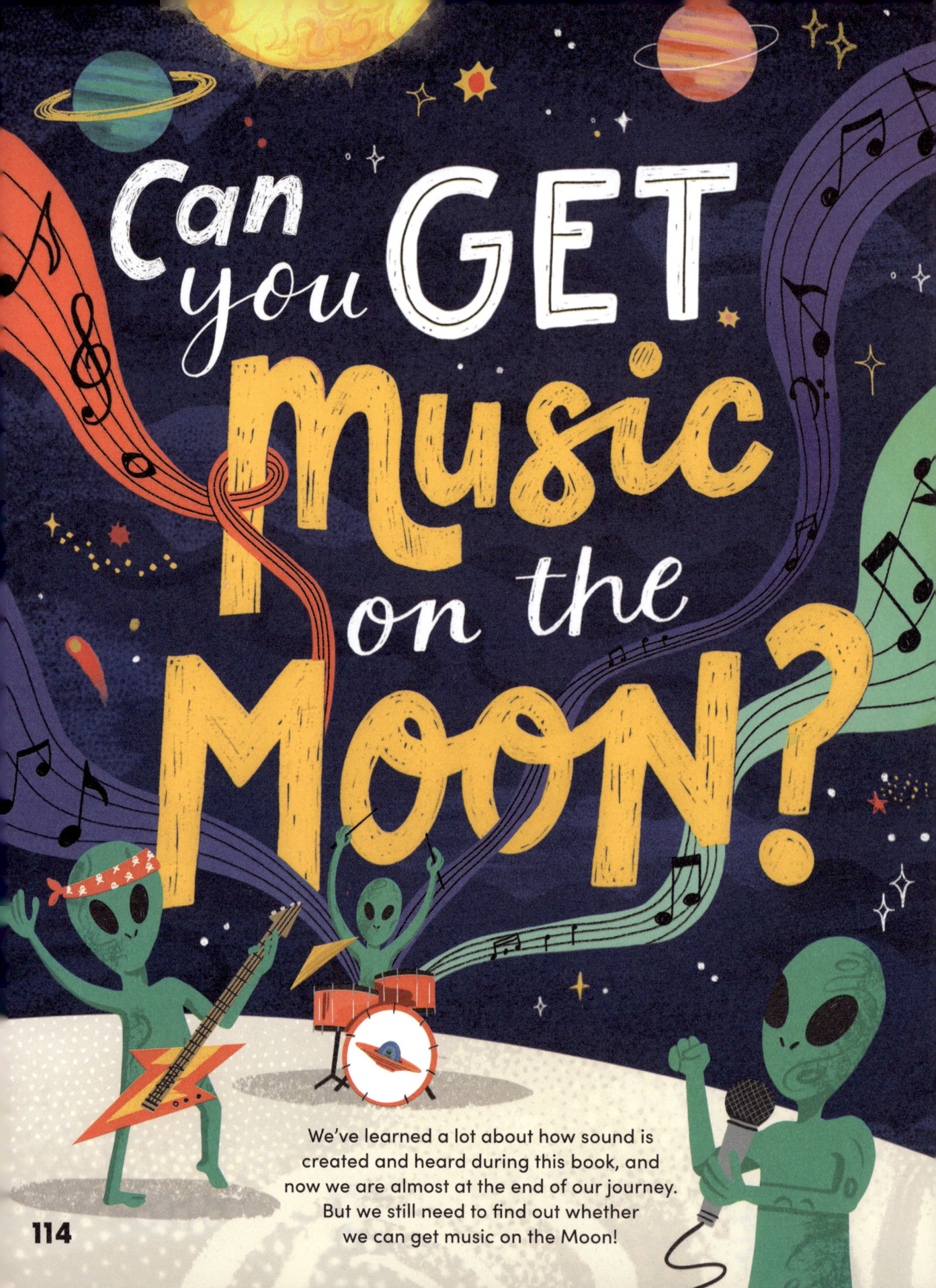

# Can you GET music on the MOON?

We've learned a lot about how sound is created and heard during this book, and now we are almost at the end of our journey. But we still need to find out whether we can get music on the Moon!

## EARTH'S MOON

Unlike Saturn with its many moons, Earth has just one moon. The Moon is a rocky place with big holes on its surface called craters, and it's about a quarter of the size of Earth. Although the Moon appears to glow in the night sky, the light doesn't actually come from the Moon itself – it's light that is reflected from the Sun. We always see the same side of the Moon from Earth because the Moon is spinning on its axis (an invisible line through its centre) at the same speed that it is orbiting the Earth. There is no atmosphere on the Moon, so the astronauts that have been there needed to wear space suits with an oxygen supply to allow them to breathe.

If you were to stand on the Moon's surface and play music, the sound wouldn't travel very well, because the Moon doesn't have an atmosphere – so there is no air for the sound to travel through. So technically no, it wouldn't be possible to hear music on the Moon. But some astronauts *did* report hearing strange sounds when they landed on the Moon – and the reason why is still a mystery!

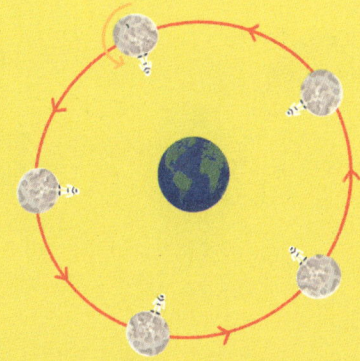

## THE DARK SIDE OF THE MOON

During the Apollo missions in the 1960s and 70s, astronauts reported strange noises and unexplained music when they travelled to the far side of the Moon (the side that we cannot see from Earth). Audio tapes from the *Apollo 10* mission in 1969 recorded astronauts talking about 'outer-space music', which stops after about an hour. As the astronauts were on the far side of the Moon at the time, they didn't have any contact with people back on Earth – they were too far away.

Michael Collins was the *Apollo 11* astronaut who stayed on board the command module *Columbia* while Neil Armstrong and Buzz Aldrin landed the lunar module *Eagle* and put the first human feet on the Moon in 1969. Collins also heard noises from the command module when it was on the far side of the Moon. Technicians back at NASA believed that these noises may have been radio interference between the command module and the lunar module, but we don't know for sure where these mysterious moon sounds came from! Who knows – maybe future missions to the Moon, such as NASA's Artemis mission, might discover the source of this moon music?

# SOUND, SPACE AND BEYOND

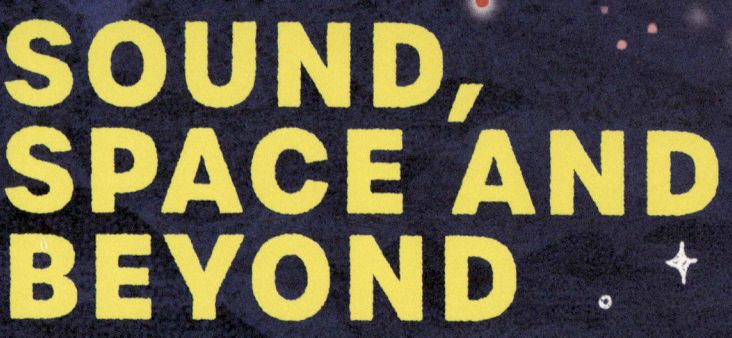

There is lots we are still learning about sound in space, and even though we might not be able to 'hear' sounds in space like we can on Earth, that doesn't mean that they don't exist. Perhaps there are other beings out there who can hear those sounds, in the same way that some animals on Earth can hear different frequencies and wavelengths from us.

So, the question of whether or not it's possible to hear in space really depends on how you define sound and hearing. What's more, turning electromagnetic waves into sound allows people with visual impairments to imagine objects or phenomena through sound, or vibrations. Audio-space projects are a way of making scientific discoveries more accessible, and they also inspire more people to 'listen up' to the stars.

After all, space really is for everyone!

SO, CAN YOU GET MUSIC ON THE MOON?

# GLOSSARY

**ACOUSTICS** a branch of physics that involves the study of sound, including the way it's produced, transmitted and received, and its effects on objects. Some of these sounds, such as ultrasound and infrasound, may be too high or low to be heard by humans.

**AMPLIFIES** increases the strength of a sound, making it louder.

**AMPLITUDE** a measurement of the height of a sound-wave. The greater the height, the stronger the wave's vibrations will be, and the louder the sound it makes.

**ATOMS** the smallest units that exist, atoms are the building blocks of all matter, including humans.

**BLACK HOLE** a region in space formed when a star dies, causing massive amounts of matter to be compressed into a small space from which nothing can escape – not even light.

**CASSETTE TAPE** a device on which music can be recorded that was invented in the early 1960s. Cassettes were much more portable than vinyl records and were popular until CDs took over in the 1990s.

**COCHLEA** a hollow, fluid-filled tube deep in your ear that is responsible for hearing. It gets its name from the Greek word for 'shell', as it looks like a coiled snail shell.

**COMPACT DISC** also called a CD, it stores digital audio and video data, and plays it by being scanned by a laser beam.

**COMPRESSION** the high pressure and high density at the peak, or crest, of a sound-wave, where particles are closer together.

**CONVECTION CURRENT** a heat-driven movement of energy caused by differences in temperature, created when warmer, thinner material rises, while cooler, denser material sinks, allowing, for example, hot-air balloons to rise.

**CUNEIFORM** a writing system made in clay tablets, widely used in the ancient Middle East around five thousand years ago. The name comes from the Latin word 'cuneus', meaning 'wedge'.

**DIAPHRAGM** a thin, flexible disk used in microphones, which vibrates in response to sound-waves. In loudspeakers, earphones and old-fashioned gramophone players, the diaphragm generates sound-waves from the vibrations.

**DIFFRACTED** when a sound-wave or light beam hits an obstacle as it travels through the air, it becomes diffracted, spreading out and changing direction.

**ECHOLOCATION** the method some animals, including dolphins and some whales and bats, use to locate objects around them. They send out sound-waves and receive the echoes that bounce back from the objects they hit, using them to create sound images of the surrounding area.

**ELECTRICITY** a form of energy that can be carried by wires and that is used to provide power to run heaters, lights and machines.

**ELECTROMAGNETIC SPECTRUM** the range of all the types of radiation, which is energy that travels in waves and has both electric and magnetic fields.

**ELECTRON** a tiny particle that has a negative charge of electricity and travels around the nucleus of an atom.

**FREQUENCY** also called 'pitch', frequency refers to the number of sound-waves there are in one second. The higher the frequency, the shorter the length of the wave will be, and the more waves there will be in one second. High-frequency sound-waves create a high-pitched noise, while low-frequency waves are more of a deep rumble.

**GRAMOPHONE** an early type of record player that played music recorded on an engraved disk.

**HELIOSEISMOLOGY** the study of the Sun's interior by observing the vibrations on its surface.

**INFRASOUND** low-frequency sound-waves that are below the range of human hearing.

**LARYNX** also called the voice box, this hollow tube in the middle of your neck contains two vocal cords and is used for breathing, swallowing and talking.